PAPER CHESS

Create your own chess set with a detachable board and 2 full sets of punch-out pieces

KELL BLACK
WITH JOHN SAUNDERS

Ivy Press

First published in the UK in 2009 by
Ivy Press
210 High Street, Lewes
East Sussex BN7 2NS, UK
www.ivy-group.co.uk

British Library Cataloguing-in-Publication Data
A catalogue record for this book is available from the British Library

ISBN: 978-1-905695-82-9

Printed in China

10 9 8 7 6 5 4 3 2 1

Ivy Press
This book was conceived, designed, and produced by Ivy Press

Creative Director Peter Bridgewater
Publisher Jason Hook
Editorial Director Tom Kitch
Art Director Wayne Blades
Designer Kate Haynes
Papercraft Instructions Kell Black
Chess Instructions John Saunders

Contents

HOW TO PLAY CHESS

Chess is probably the world's most famous board game. It is certainly the most widespread, being played on every continent and in almost every country on the planet. The rules have remained unchanged since the late sixteenth century and a system for recording the moves dates back even further, allowing chess aficionados to follow and appreciate the expertise of medieval players. Chess is played by huge numbers of people worldwide, including some hundreds of professionals as well as millions of competition players and still more who play the game purely for fun.

Despite the advent of computer games that can compete on equal terms with world champions, programmers are still a long way from "solving" the game's intricacies—and yet children can easily learn the rules at a very early age. Chess has occasionally produced prodigies who can play at expert level well under the age of 10, but chess is also simple enough to be played with huge enjoyment by almost everyone. This wide spectrum of appeal is probably the secret of its universal popularity.

A game of chess is played by two players on the same eight-by-eight board that is used for checkers, with 32 white and 32 black squares. Unlike checkers, all 64 squares of the board are utilized in the playing of chess. There are 16 pieces (often referred to as "men") of six different types, each with unique powers of movement, in each player's initial line-up. Players take turns to move one of their pieces from one square to another, with the player having the white pieces always making the first move of the game. If a piece is moved to a square currently occupied by an enemy piece, it displaces or "takes" that piece, which is removed from the game.

The object of the game is to "checkmate" the opponent. This entails making a move that attacks the opponent's most important piece—the king—so that it has no reply that escapes the attack (or attack from other pieces) or otherwise allows it to evade the attack by blocking or capturing the attacking piece. When a king is attacked and has no escape, it has been checkmated and the game ends immediately in favor of the player who has played the checkmating move.

If the king is attacked by an enemy piece but has at least one move that allows it to escape attack, it is said to be "in check." This is not the end of the game, but the defending player is obliged by the rules to make a move that escapes the check on that turn. Chess games can also end in a draw. If a situation arises where a player can make no legal move with any remaining piece, or where a king's move would expose it to attack—but the king is not currently in check—then the game ends immediately in a draw or "stalemate."

Over the next six pages you will discover how each piece is used in chess. Pages eleven to sixteen contain instructions for making the chess pieces.

MAKING THE PIECES

Tools The tools required for making the chess pieces are simple and few. You need white PVA glue, toothpicks, tweezers, a straightedge ruler, and an empty ballpoint pen or a small butter knife. An emery board is also useful but it's not essential. Most of all you need patience, time, and a small but clear space in which to work.

Pieces The chess pieces have been die-cut for easy removal from their pages. Gently press them out. If a few tufts of paper remain along the edges you can remove them with a few light strokes with an emery board.

Scoring Before you attempt to fold the pieces you will need to score along the fold lines. To do this, place your straightedge ruler along the line of the fold, hold it firmly in place with one hand, and run the tip of the empty ballpoint pen or the blunt edge of the butter knife against it to score along the fold. This will compress the paper's fibers and the piece will fold neatly along this slight crease.

Assembly The pieces are designed to be put together as easily as possible, however they are small and they do require a bit of care, so take your time. This is a process to be enjoyed and savored.

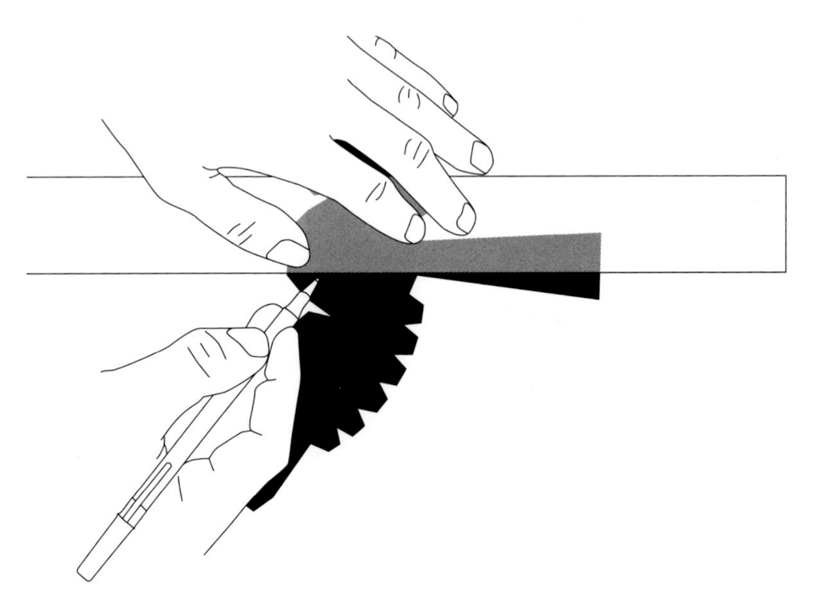

Read all the instructions carefully and follow the steps in sequence. Dry fit all the elements before applying glue. Remember, one dot glues a lot and using too much glue will warp the paper. Use the toothpicks to apply the glue to the tabs and hold the join together for around twenty seconds while the glue is drying. Use tweezers to reach into the small spots. Remember, take your time and keep your work area neat.

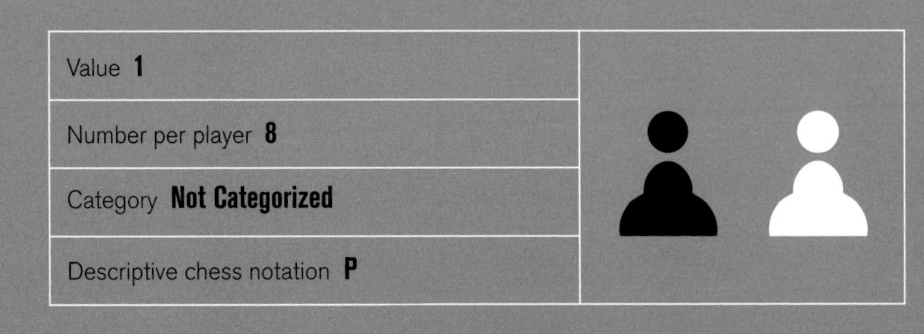

Value **1**	
Number per player **8**	
Category **Not Categorized**	
Descriptive chess notation **P**	

Pawn

The common saying, "only a pawn in the game," is derived from the fact that a pawn is the humblest piece on the chessboard. However, it is also numerous—each player starts with eight pawns—and it is a mark of a good player to treat the pawns with respect.

The pawn can only move forward. It moves along the file (a row of vertical squares) one square at a time, except on its first move when it can move two squares forward. Where there is a piece on the square in front, it remains immobilized. However, the pawn captures one square forward diagonally. It is permitted one further type of capture, called "en passant." It is allowed to capture an opposing pawn making an initial two-square move as if the enemy pawn had only moved one square. The capturing pawn is placed on the square the captured pawn would have occupied had it only advanced one square. This can only be done on the turn immediately following the opposing pawn's two-square advance.

Though an individual pawn is the least valuable of a player's army, three pawns together are worth a knight or a bishop. The pawn's value rises hugely if it succeeds in reaching the opposition back rank unscathed, as it is then promoted—that is, replaced by a new queen, rook, bishop, or knight, as its owner chooses.

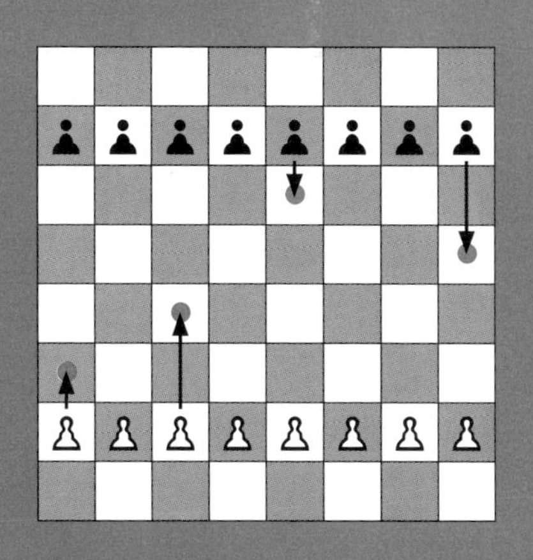

Above The pawns' starting positions, showing one-square and two-square initial moves. Any pawn can make the first move.

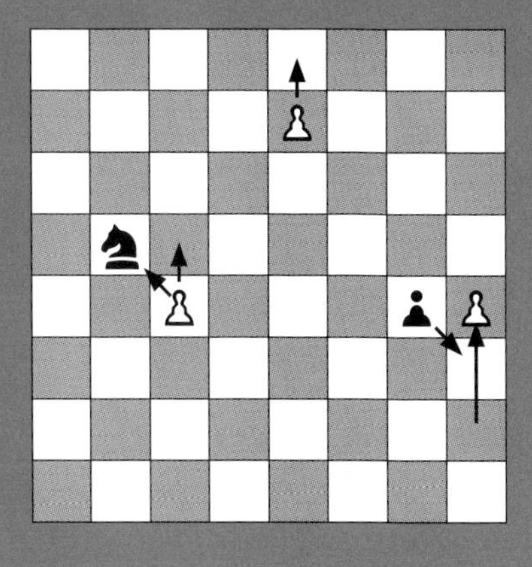

Left The white pawn on the left can either capture the knight or move one square forward. The black pawn on the right can capture "en passant" the white pawn that has just moved two squares forward on its last move. The white pawn is removed and the capturing black pawn placed on the white square behind it. The white pawn nearest the opposition end can move to the white square and be promoted to a queen, rook, bishop, or knight.

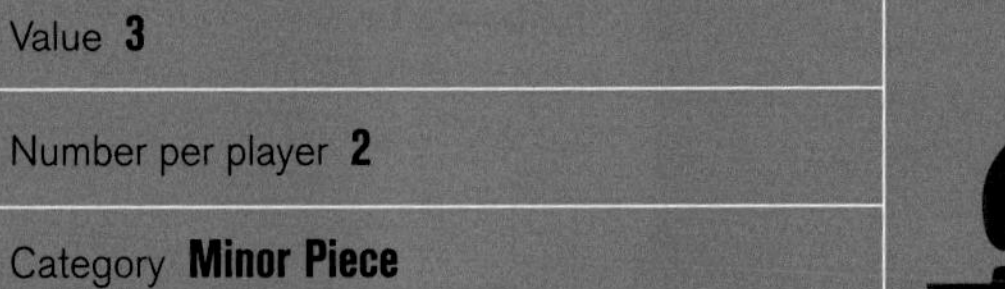

Value **3**	
Number per player **2**	
Category **Minor Piece**	
Descriptive chess notation **B**	

Bishop

The bishop is a piece of middling value on the chessboard. It moves along diagonals by as many squares as the player wishes, so long as it is not impeded by another piece—although it can capture an enemy piece that blocks its path. Each player starts the game with two bishops, one on a black square and one on a white.

Because it moves diagonally, a bishop can only move to squares of the same color as the square the bishop started the game on. This makes it significantly less valuable than a rook, which has access to all 64 squares on the board. However, it traverses the board rather quicker than the knight, so it is roughly of equal value to that piece. Two bishops with open lines can command many squares and are more than a match for a rook. Bishops often enter the battle at an early stage, as their oblique moves can take them through the lines of pawns. If supported by a queen or knight, they can initiate a swift attack on an unsuspecting enemy king.

A player left with only a bishop to accompany the king against a lone enemy king is unable to give checkmate, so the game must be abandoned as a draw. However, two bishops can effect a mate, as can a bishop and a knight, though both these operations need a good deal of skill and practice.

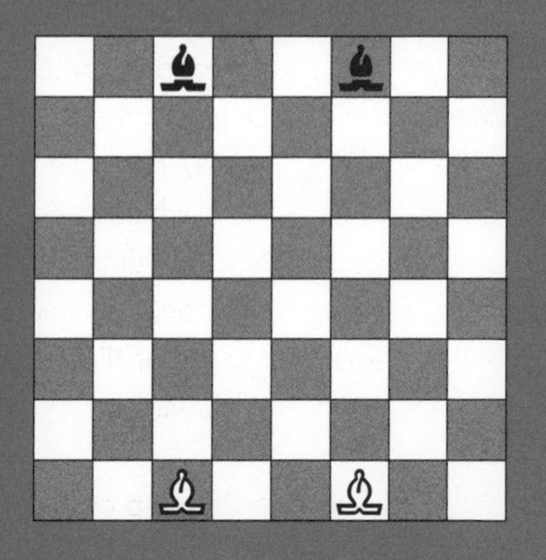

Above The bishops on their initial squares.

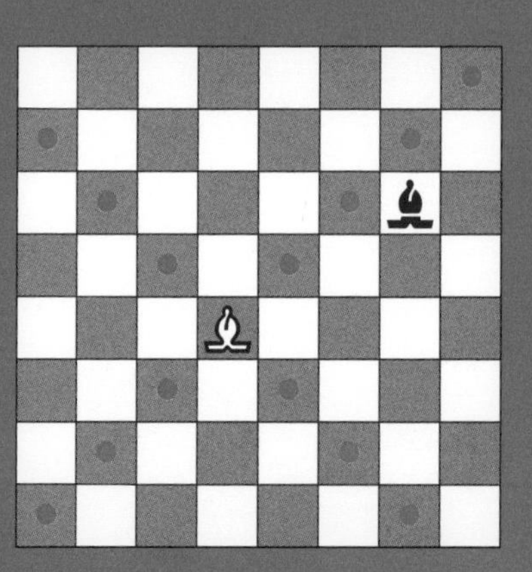

Left The white bishop's available moves are shown. Note that it can never cross the path of one the black bishops, which operates exclusively on the white squares.

Value **3**	
Number per player **2**	
Category **Minor Piece**	
Descriptive chess notation **N or Kt**	

Knight

The knight's move is like no other on the chessboard and, uniquely, it is permitted to jump over other pieces (whether friend or foe). Its move can be summarized as a move to the nearest square which is not on the same rank, file (a row of horizontal squares), or diagonal on which it currently stands. Some players find it easier to think of the move as an "L" shape—two squares along rank or file, followed by a 90-degree turn left or right to the next square.

The knight's ability to jump over other pieces gives it added maneuverability in many crowded chessboard situations but it takes several hops to traverse the board. Hence its value is significantly below the queen's or a rook's, and about equal to a bishop's.

The knight's move is not permitted to the queen, so it can prove deadly in situations where it gives check to the king and simultaneously attacks the opposing queen. Such a move is called a "fork" and is often ruinous to the side on whom it is inflicted.

Knights operate best with plenty of space. In the middle of the board they can command (or attack) as many as eight squares, but on the edge of the board their influence can be much reduced.

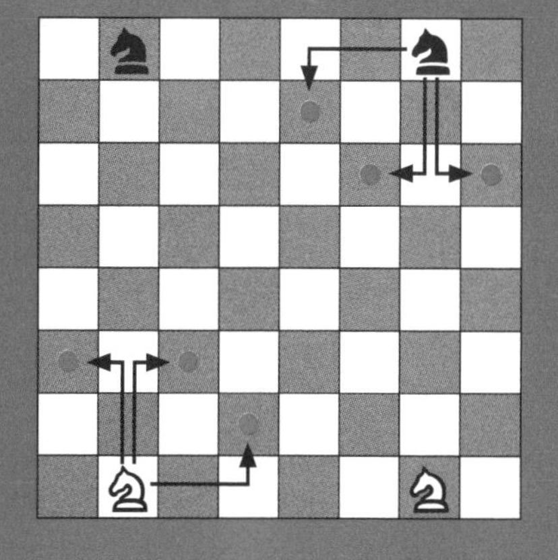

Above The knights on their initial squares. Also shown are possible moves for the white and black knights.

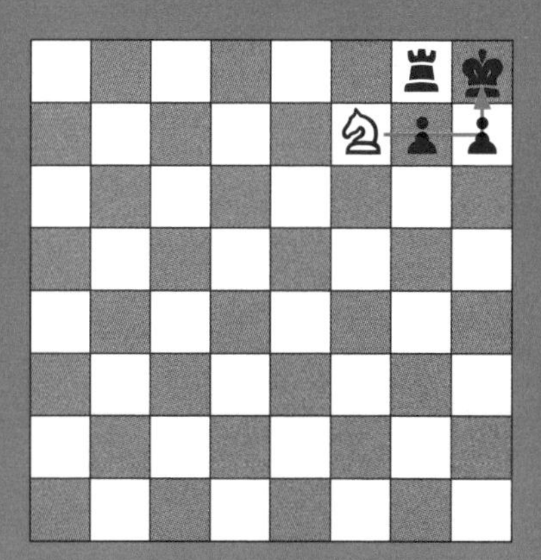

Left The knight can jump over other pieces. Here, a lone knight gives checkmate to the opposing king, which is blocked in by its own pieces. This is called a "smothered mate."

Value **5**	
Number per player **2**	
Category **Major Piece**	
Descriptive chess notation **R**	

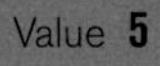

Rook

The rook (sometimes wrongly referred to by players who are new to chess as the "castle") is the second-most powerful piece after the queen in most chessboard situations. It can move to any square along the file or rank on which it is already situated unless it is blocked by another piece.

Despite its potency, the rook tends to take a back seat in the initial stages of the game because its scope is impeded by its own pawns and other pieces. It comes into its own later in the game, particularly when an open file becomes available—that is, when the player's own pawn has disappeared from a file and it is possible to attack the enemy army directly along the opened line. The rook has a special move called "castling," which is made in conjunction with the king (see page 10).

If a player is left with only a rook to accompany the king, it is still possible—and quite easy with some practice—to checkmate a lone enemy king. The rook and king work in tandem to force the enemy king to the edge of the board, where checkmate can be delivered. In this regard, the lone rook is markedly superior to a single bishop or knight, neither of which can force checkmate when they are left as the king's only companion.

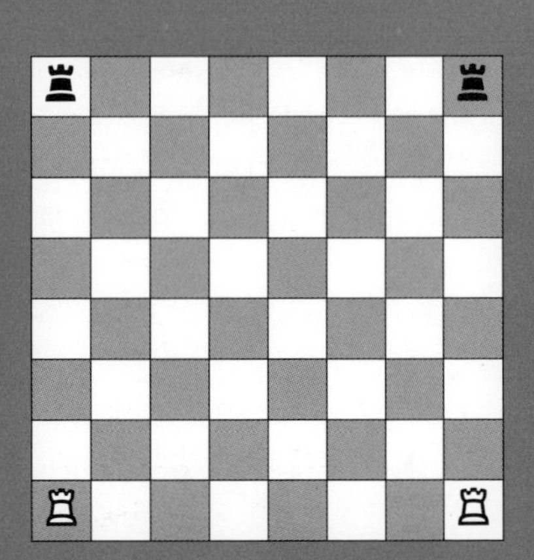

Above The rooks' starting positions.

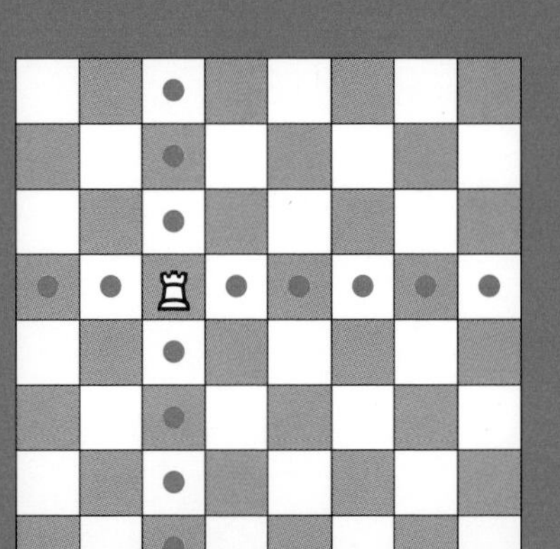

Left The rook can move along ranks or files but not diagonally. It can move any number of squares unless blocked by another piece. It cannot jump over other pieces.

Value **9**
Number per player **1**
Category **Major Piece**
Descriptive chess notation **Q**

Queen

The queen is not the most important piece on the board (that honor belongs to the king); however, it is the most powerful. Its move combines those of rook and bishop: it can move any number of squares along rank, file, or diagonal unless blocked by another piece. It can capture an enemy piece that lies in its direct path along any of these lines.

Each player starts the game with only one queen, which resides initially on a square of its own color beside the king. Though powerful, it is often a mistake to launch the queen in the initial stages of a game in case it is trapped or ambushed by well-coordinated enemy pieces. Because of its great value, the loss of the queen is likely to lead to swift defeat. More able players often advance their less-valuable pieces first and only bring the queen into the battle when it can be supported by well-posted allies.

A new queen can be acquired later in a game by means of a pawn being promoted. Though other, lesser pieces can be chosen, the player who promotes a pawn nearly always chooses to promote it to a queen. A player left with just a queen to accompany the king against a lone enemy king can still achieve checkmate, and the technique is relatively simple to master.

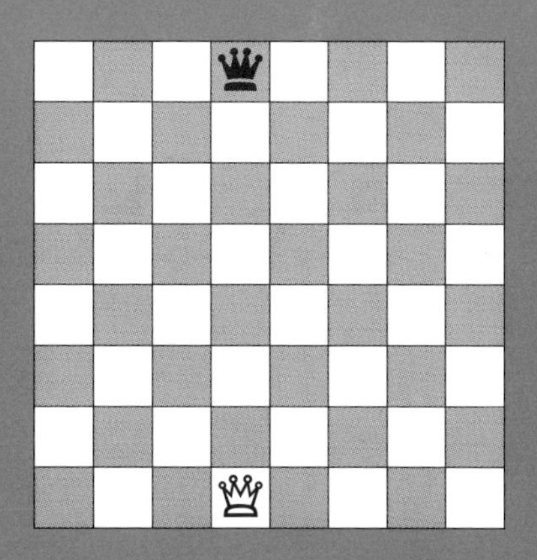

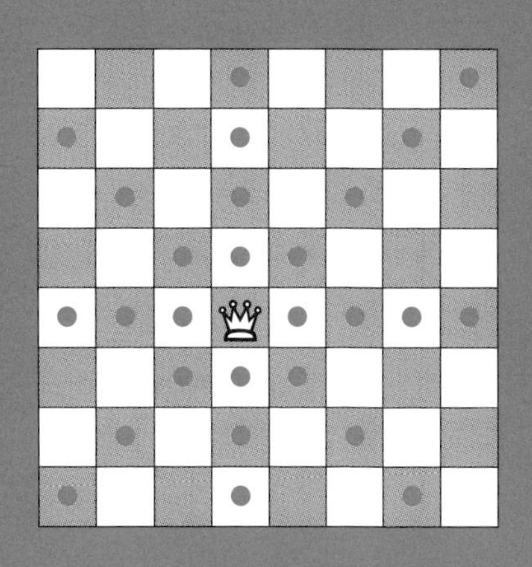

Above The two queens on their initial squares. They are placed on squares of their own color. The board must be oriented with the rightmost square nearest each player being white (hence the saying "right is white").

Left A queen in the middle of the board can reach as many as 27 different squares.

Value **Infinite**	
Number per player **1**	
Category **Not Categorized**	
Descriptive chess notation **K**	

King

The king can move in any direction along rank, file, or diagonal, but only one square at a time. It takes a long time to traverse the board so it is relatively weak compared with the other pieces. It has great difficulty in escaping an attacking force of enemy pieces. However, its value is infinite, as the king's fate (or that of its opposite number) decides the result of the game.

Often the best strategy early in the game is to hide the king away behind a defensive line of pawns. There is a special move called "castling" involving a move of the king and a rook on the same turn. Where neither have previously moved, there are no pieces on the intervening squares, and none of the squares in the king's path (including its initial square) are attacked by the opposition, the king is allowed to move two squares along the rank toward a rook, and the rook is moved either two squares if it's the rook on the king's side of the board, or three squares if it's the rook on the queen's side of the board. The former is known as "kingside" castling, the latter "queenside" castling.

Kings can capture opposition pieces but can be blocked in by their own pieces. The kings are not permitted to attack each other, to be adjacent to each other, or move to a square that is under attack.

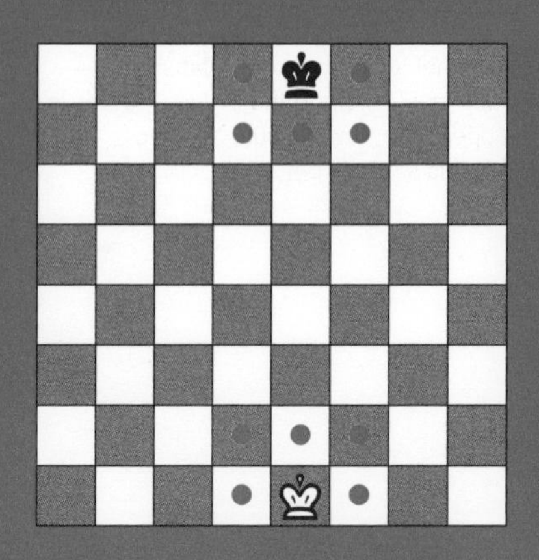

Above The kings on their initial squares. They can move one square in any direction.

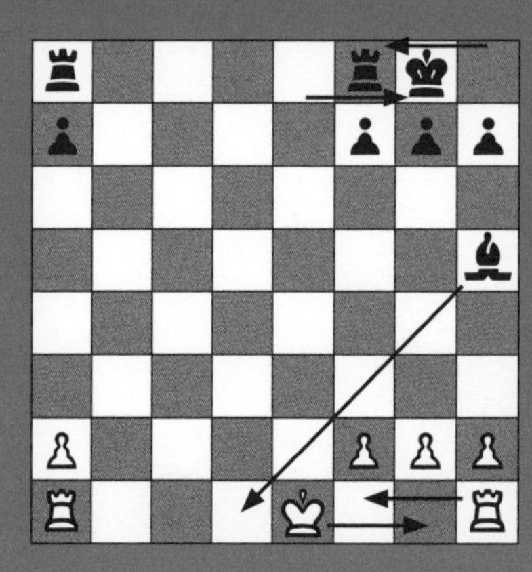

Left Castling is only permitted if the king and rook involved have not previously moved in the game. Here, the black king and rook have just castled, moving from their initial squares to either side of each other. White is permitted to do the same, on the same side of the board ("the kingside"), but cannot currently do so on the left side ("the queenside") because it would involve passing over a square attacked by the black bishop.

Making the Pawn

Step 1 To make the pawn, start with the lower base. Fold the sides inward on the fold lines. Glue the six small gray triangular tabs to the insides of their neighboring sides, creating a six-sided open box. Glue a small coin inside the box.

Step 2 Fold the pawn's upper base on the fold lines and glue it together by the one large gray tab.

Step 3 Fold the stem on the fold lines and glue the long gray tab to the inside of the opposite edge.

Step 4 Take the stem and fold the six gray tabs outward on the dotted lines. Put a drop of glue on each tab and slide the stem upward through the inside of the upper base until you've created a funnel. Gently press the tabs of the pawn's stem to the inside of the upper base, making sure that the stem is straight. Let dry.

Step 5 Put a drop of glue on each of the lower base's six tabs. Align the upper base and stem to the pawn's lower base and carefully attach them together, making sure that the tabs are glued to the insides of their opposite pieces.

Step 6 Assemble the pawn's head by gluing the gray end tabs to their opposites, creating two hinged hexagonal funnels. Let dry. Glue the five triangular gray tabs on the lower half of the head to the inside of the upper half as shown.

Step 7 Glue the completed head to the stem and collar to finish creating your pawn.

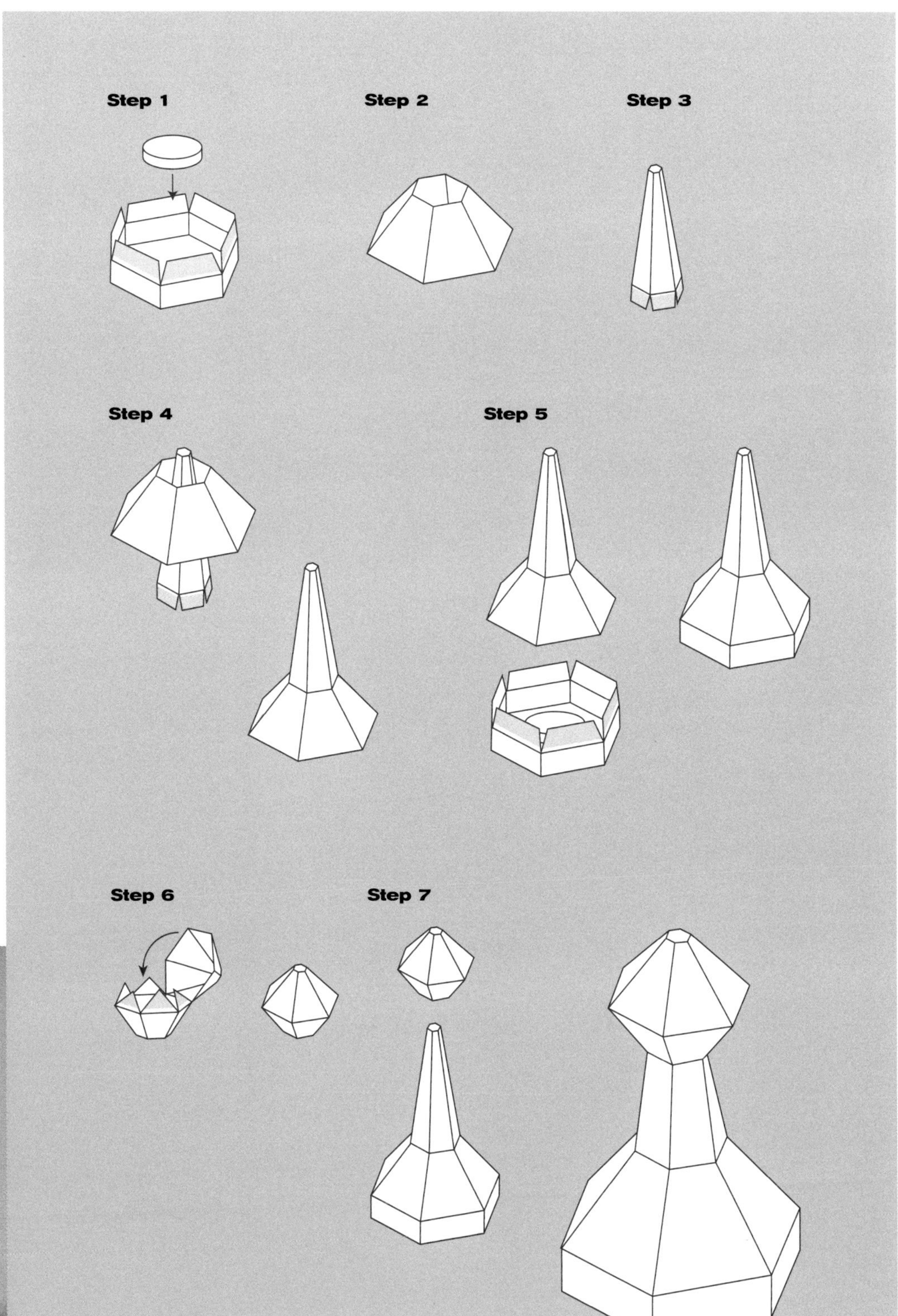

Making the Bishop

Step 1 To make the bishop, start with the lower base. Fold the sides inward on the fold lines. Glue the six small gray triangular tabs to the insides of their neighboring sides, creating a six-sided open box. Glue a small coin inside the box.

Step 2 Fold the upper base on the fold lines and glue it together by the one large gray tab.

Step 3 Fold the stem on the fold lines and glue the long gray tab to the inside of the opposite edge.

Step 4 Take the stem and fold the six gray tabs outward on the dotted lines. Put a drop of glue on each tab and slide the stem upward through the inside of the upper base until you've created a funnel. Gently press the tabs of the bishop's stem to the inside of the upper base, making sure that the stem is straight. Let dry.

Step 5 Put a drop of glue on each of the six tabs on the lower base. Align the upper base and stem to the lower base and carefully attach them together, making sure that the tabs are glued to the insides of their opposite pieces.

Step 6 Curl the bishop's collar support on the edge of a table several times. Put a drop of glue on the end of the collar support and attach it to the gray area. Let it dry for several minutes and then carefully wrap the rest of the strip around the stem. Add a tiny dot of glue every inch (2.5cm).

Step 7 Glue the bishop's collar to the collar support and stem.

Step 8 Assemble the miter by gluing the gray end tabs to their opposites, creating two hinged hexagonal funnels. Let dry. Glue the five triangular gray tabs on the lower half of the bishop's miter to the inside of the upper half as shown.

Step 9 Glue the completed miter to the stem and collar. Roll up and glue the button to the top of the miter to complete your bishop.

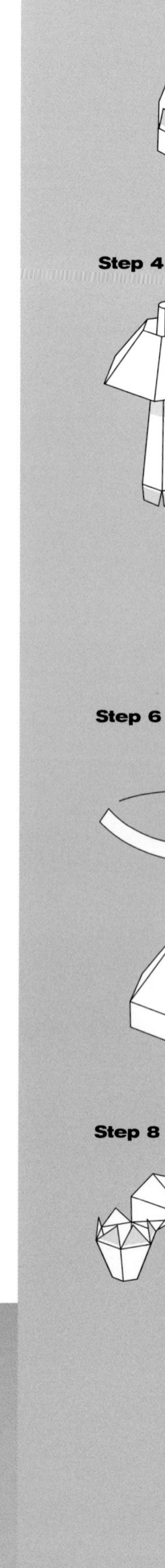

Step 1

Step 2

Step 3

Step 4

Step 5

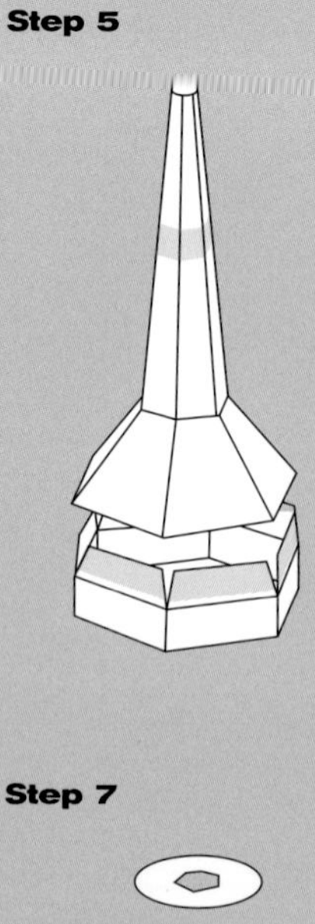

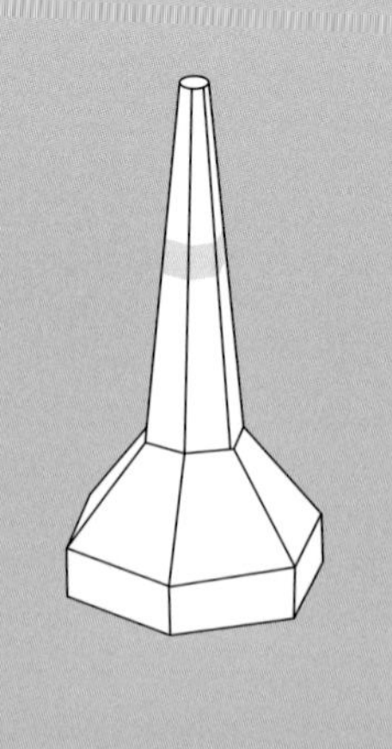

Step 6

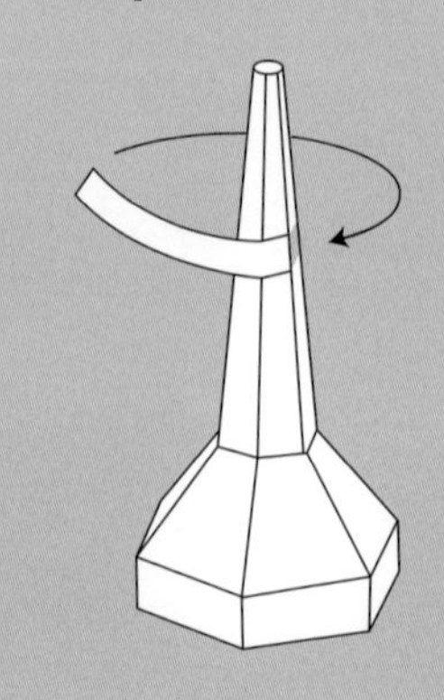

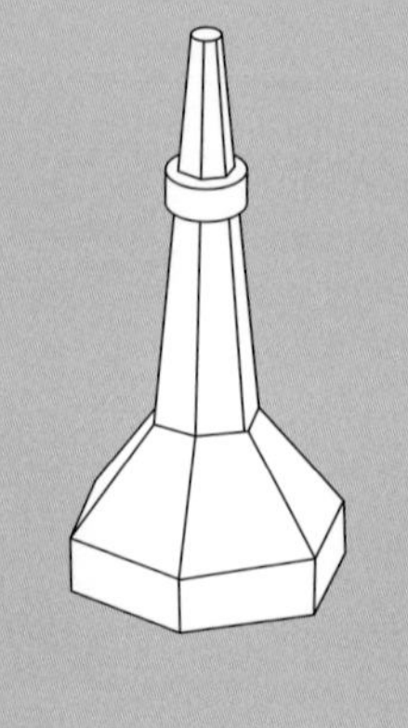

Step 7

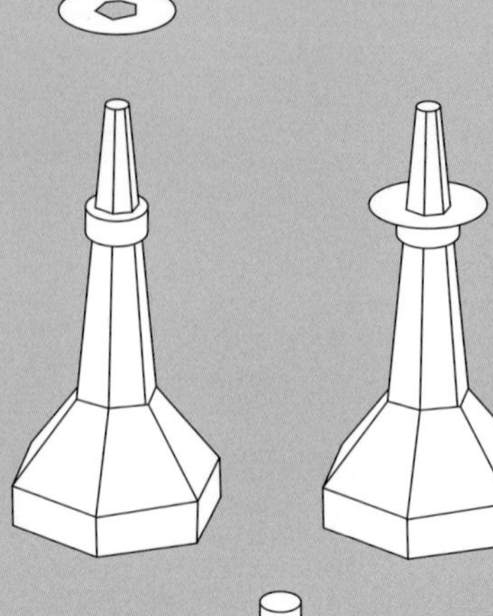

Step 8

Step 9

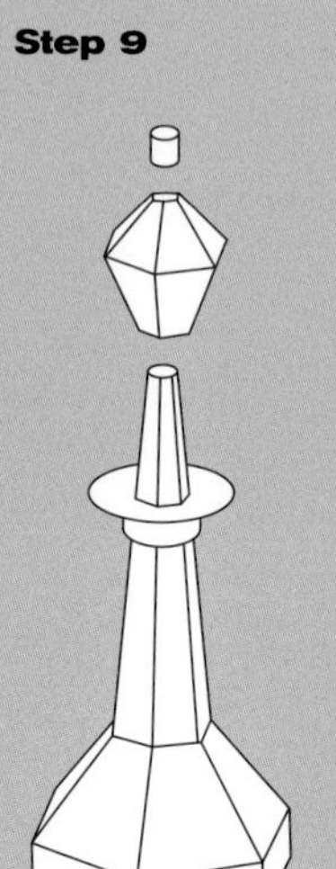

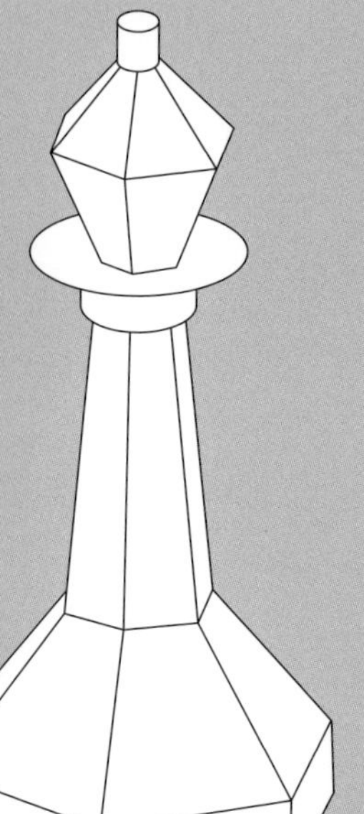

Making the Knight

The knight is slightly more difficult to assemble than the other pieces. As always, take your time and dry fit the pieces before gluing.

Step 1 Start with the lower base. Fold the sides inward on the fold lines. Glue the six small gray triangular tabs to the insides of their neighboring sides, creating a six-sided open box. Glue a small coin inside the knight's lower base.

Step 2 Fold the upper base on the fold lines and glue it together by the one large gray tab, creating what looks like a hexagonal lampshade with a lid. Fold the lid over and glue it to the five triangular tabs. Let dry.

Step 3 Glue the knight's lower base to the upper base by aligning the tabs as shown. Remember that the tabs are glued to the insides of their opposite pieces.

Step 4 The horse is next. Fold the two profiles of the horse downward toward each other. Now fold the base and attach its tab to the inside of the opposite profile. Glue the horse's snout and the top of its head into place with the triangular tabs. Carefully glue the back of the horse closed. You will find it helpful to reach in through the front of the horse to press the tabs to the back. A chopstick or the eraser end of a pencil will work well for this. Let dry.

Step 5 Glue the front of the horse to the tabs as shown to close the body.

Step 6 Glue the base to the bottom of the horse. Use the gray hexagon on the horse's underside as a guide. Let dry.

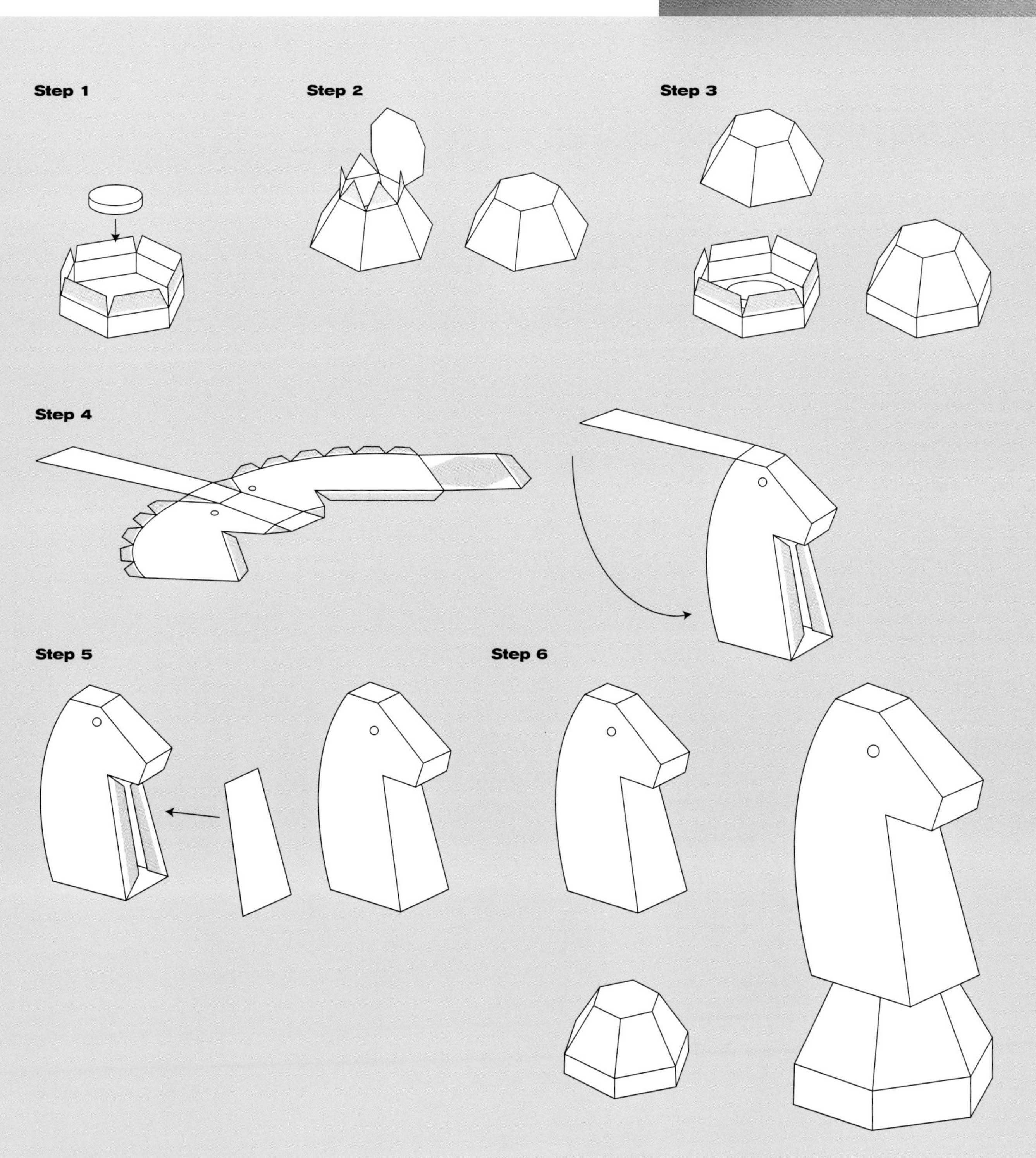

Making the Rook

Step 1 To make the rook, start with the lower base. Fold the sides inward on the fold lines. Glue the six small gray triangular tabs to the insides of their neighboring sides, creating a six-sided open box. Glue a small coin inside the lower base.

Step 2 Fold the rook's upper base on the fold lines and glue it together by the one large gray tab, creating what looks like a hexagonal lampshade.

Step 3 Next, make the rook's stem. Fold on the indicated lines and glue the long gray tab to the inside of its opposite. This creates a stocky cone. Close the top of the cone by folding over the hexagonal top piece and gluing the five triangular tabs to its underside.

Step 4 Take the stem and fold the six gray tabs outward on the dotted lines. Put a drop of glue on each tab and slide the stem upward through the inside of the upper base until you've created a kind of funnel. Gently press the tabs of the rook's stem to the inside of the upper base, making sure that the stem is straight. Let dry.

Step 5 Glue the rook's lower base to the upper base and stem component by aligning the tabs as shown. Remember that the tabs are glued to the insides of their opposite pieces.

Step 6 Create the rook's distinctive parapet by folding the sides and gluing the five triangular tabs to the inside of the hexagonal piece. Let dry.

Step 7 Glue the completed parapet to the rook's stem.

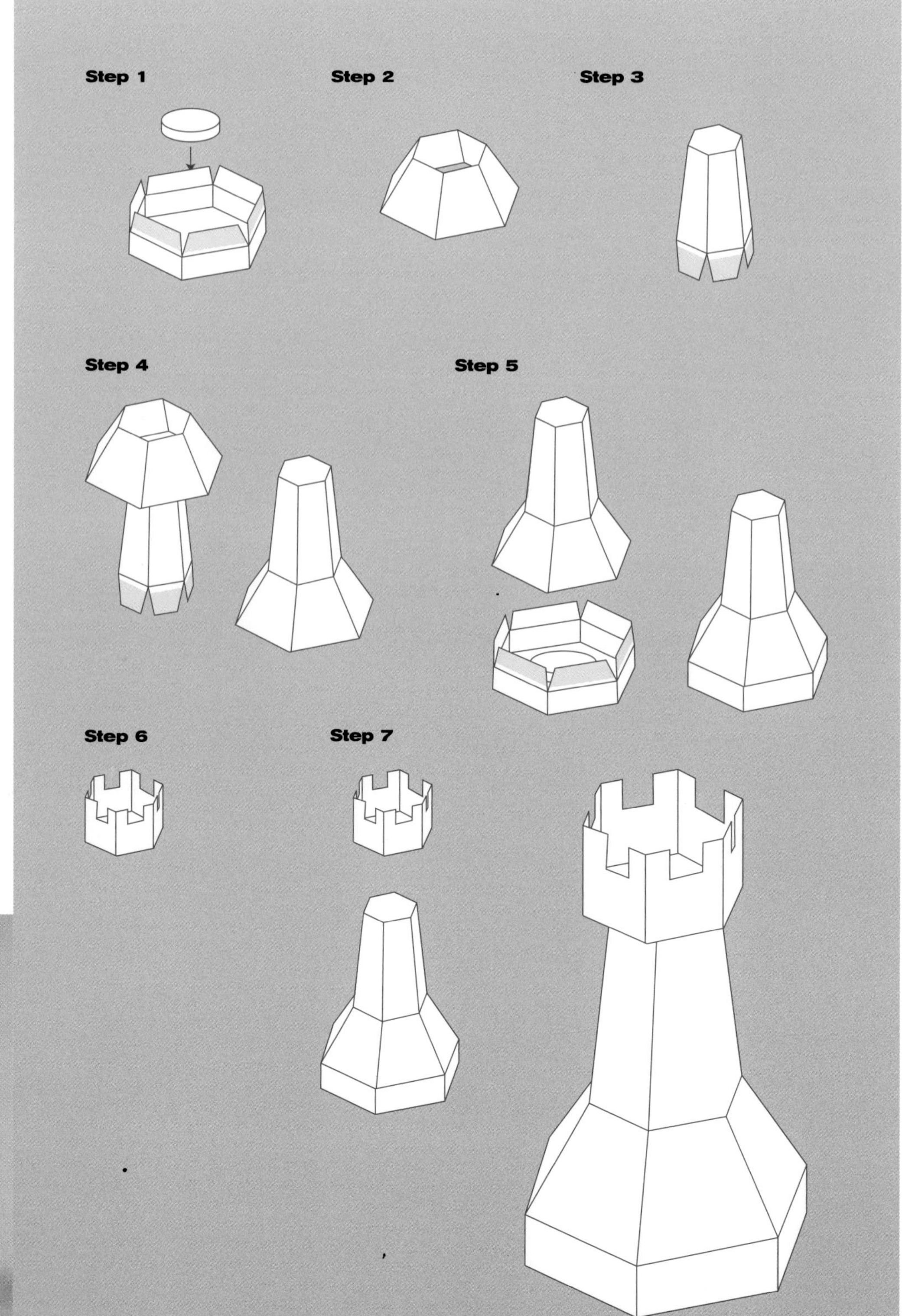

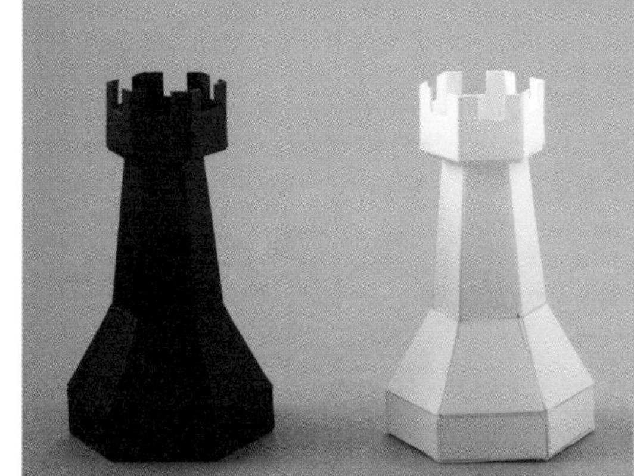

Making the Queen

Step 1 To make the queen, start with the lower base. Fold the sides inward on the fold lines. Glue the six small gray triangular tabs to the insides of their neighboring sides, creating a six-sided open box. Glue a small coin inside the lower base.

Step 2 Fold the queen's upper base on the fold lines and glue it together by the one large gray tab, creating what looks like a hexagonal lampshade.

Step 3 Next, make the queen's stem. Fold on the indicated lines and glue the long gray tab to the inside of its opposite. This creates a long cone.

Step 4 Take the stem and fold the six gray tabs outward on the dotted lines. Put a drop of glue on each tab and slide the stem upward through the inside of the upper base until you've created a funnel. Gently press the tabs of the queen's stem to the inside of the upper base, making sure that the stem is straight. Let dry.

Step 5 Glue the lower base to the upper base and stem component by aligning the tabs as shown. Remember that the tabs are glued to the insides of their opposite pieces.

Step 6 Curl the queen's collar support on the edge of a table several times. Put a drop of glue on the end of the collar support and attach it to the gray area. Let it dry for several minutes and then carefully wrap the rest of the strip around the stem. Add a tiny dot of glue every inch (2.5cm).

Step 7 Glue the queen's collar to the collar support and stem.

Step 8 Assemble the crown by gluing the gray end tab to its opposite. Create the crown insert by first assembling the hexagonal funnel and then attaching its hinged base to the upper section with the five triangular gray tabs. When dry, apply a thin bead of glue to the insert and nestle it in the queen's crown. Let dry.

Step 9 Glue the completed crown to the stem and collar. Roll up and glue the button to the top of the crown. The queen is finished.

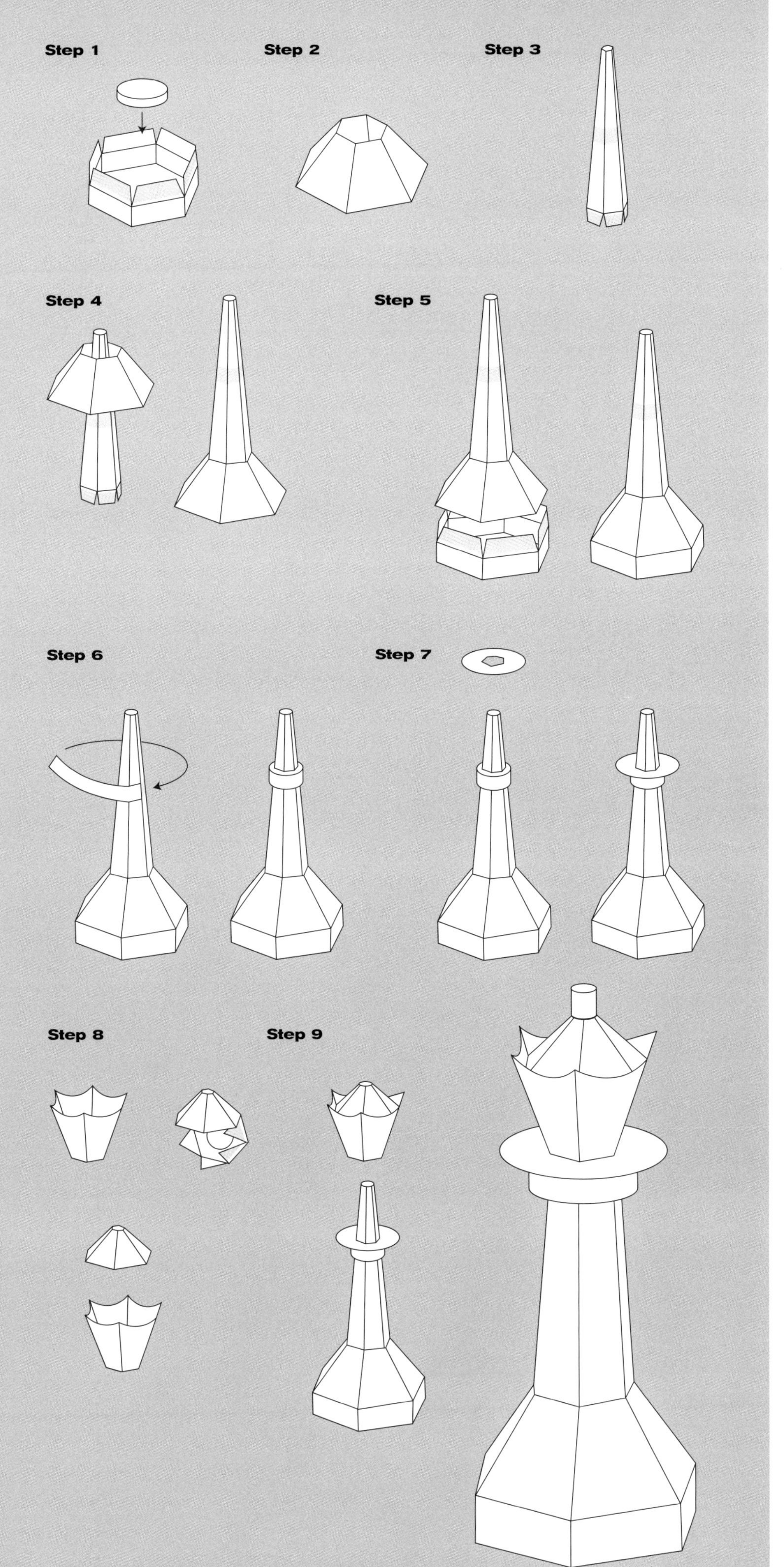

Making the King

Step 1 To make the king, start with the lower base. Fold the sides inward on the fold lines. Glue the six small gray triangular tabs to the insides of their neighboring sides, creating a six-sided open box. Glue a small coin inside the lower base.

Step 2 Fold the king's upper base on the fold lines and glue it together by the large gray tab, creating what looks like a hexagonal lampshade.

Step 3 Next, make the king's stem. Fold on the lines and glue the long gray tab to the inside of its opposite. This creates a long cone.

Step 4 Take the stem and fold the six gray tabs outward on the dotted lines. Put a drop of glue on each tab and slide the stem upward through the inside of the upper base until you've created a funnel. Gently press the tabs of the king's stem to the inside of the upper base, making sure that the stem is straight. Let dry.

Step 5 Glue the king's lower base to the upper base and stem component by aligning the tabs as shown. Remember that the tabs are glued to the insides of their opposite pieces.

Step 6 Curl the king's collar support on the edge of a table several times. Put a drop of glue on the end of the collar support and attach it to the gray area. Let dry for several minutes and then carefully wrap the rest of the strip around the stem. Add a tiny dot of glue every inch (2.5cm).

Step 7 Glue the king's collar to the collar support and stem.

Step 8 Assemble the crown by gluing the gray end tabs to their opposites, creating two hinged hexagonal funnels. When dry, glue the five triangular gray tabs on the lower half of the crown to the inside of the upper half as shown. Glue the top of the crown to the rest of the crown using the six glue tabs.

Step 9 Glue the king's completed crown to the stem and collar. Assemble the cross by folding the two halves on their dotted lines and gluing them spine-to-spine. Use just a tiny amount of glue on the spines. When dry, attach to the top of the king's crown with a dot of glue.

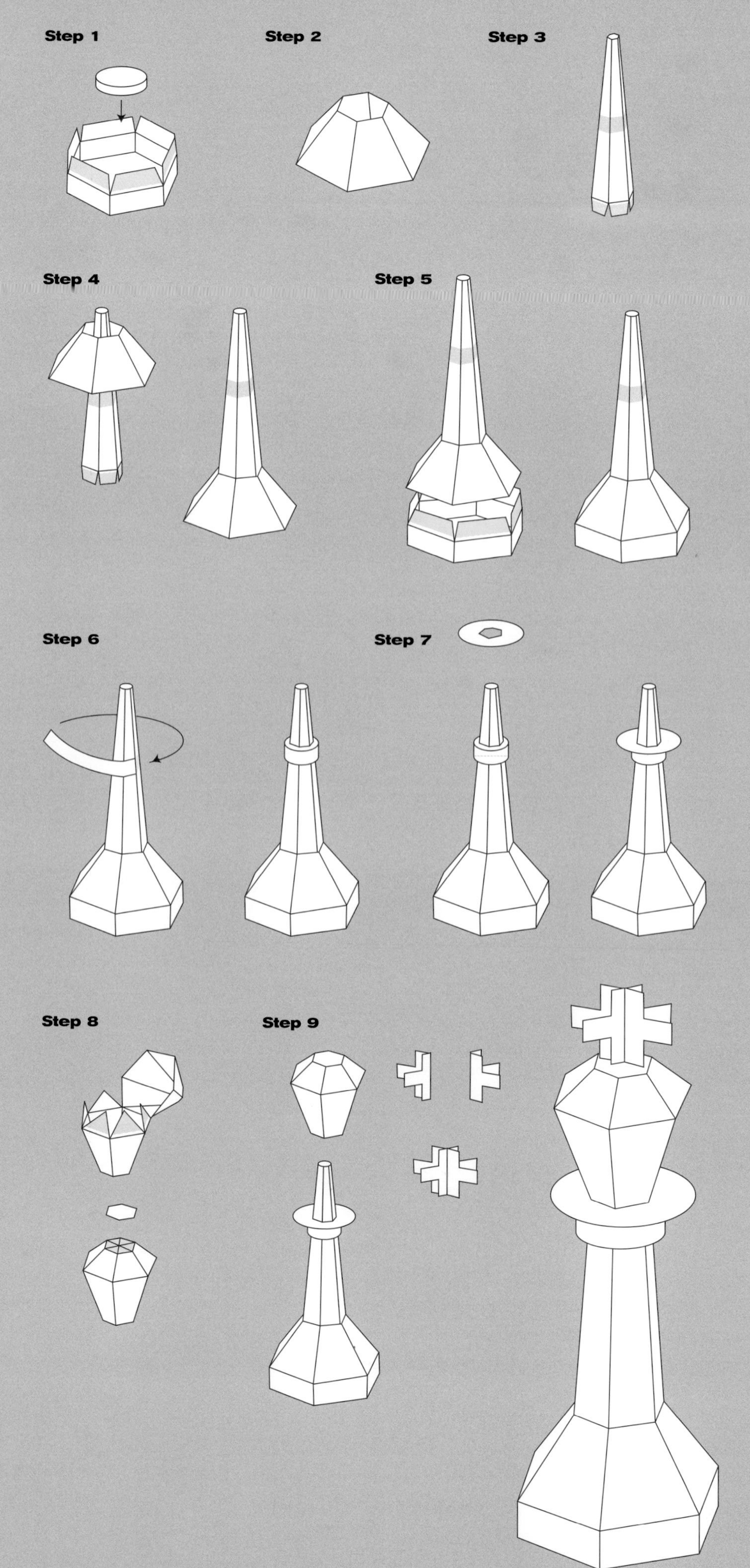

THE TEMPLATES

The White Pawns

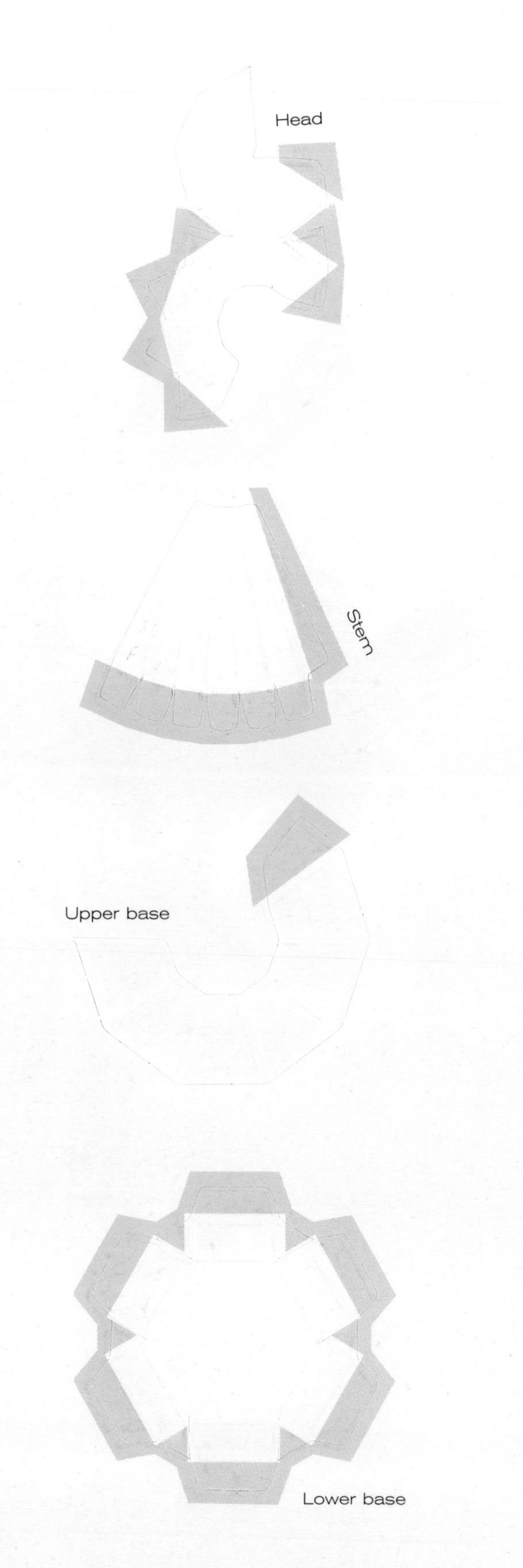

White Pawn 1

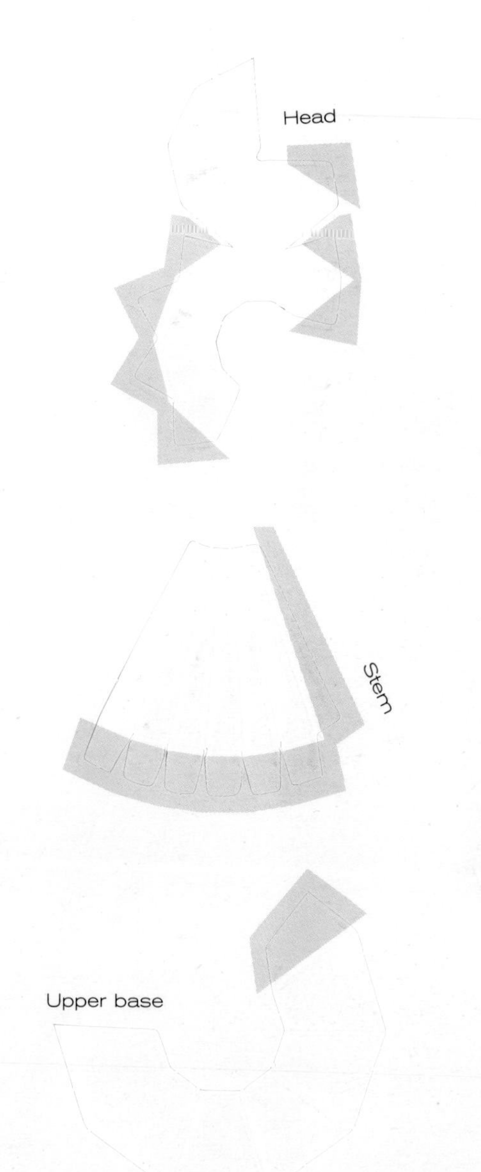

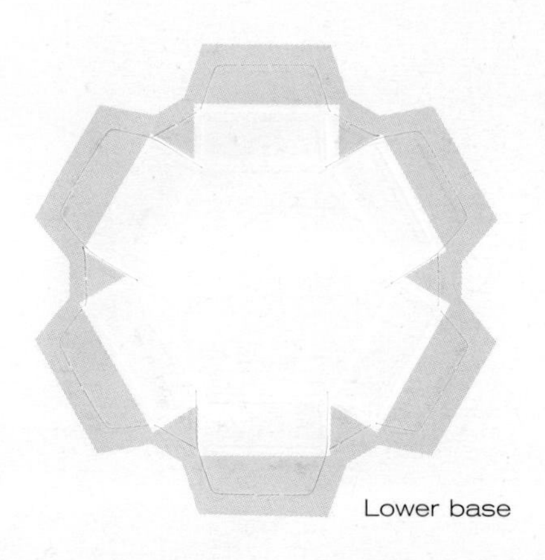

White Pawn 2

The White Pawns

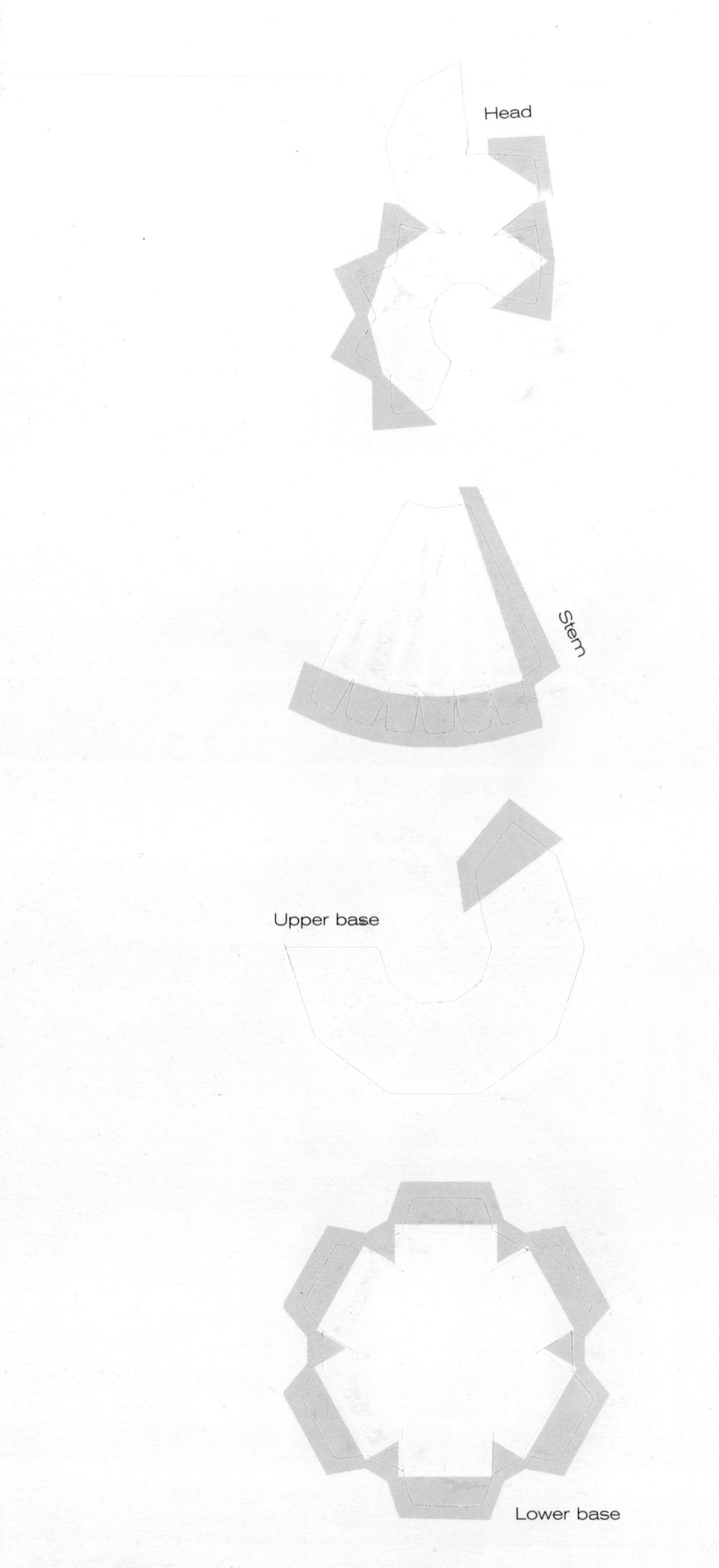

White Pawn 3

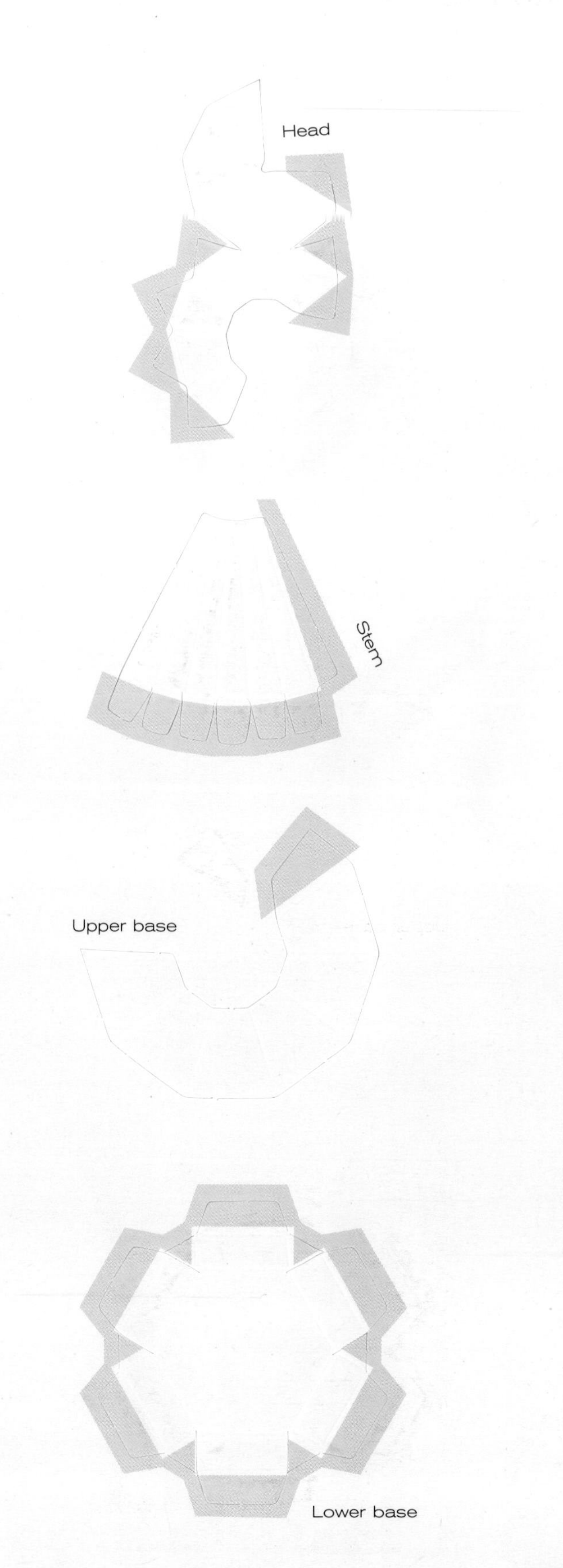

White Pawn 4

The White Pawns

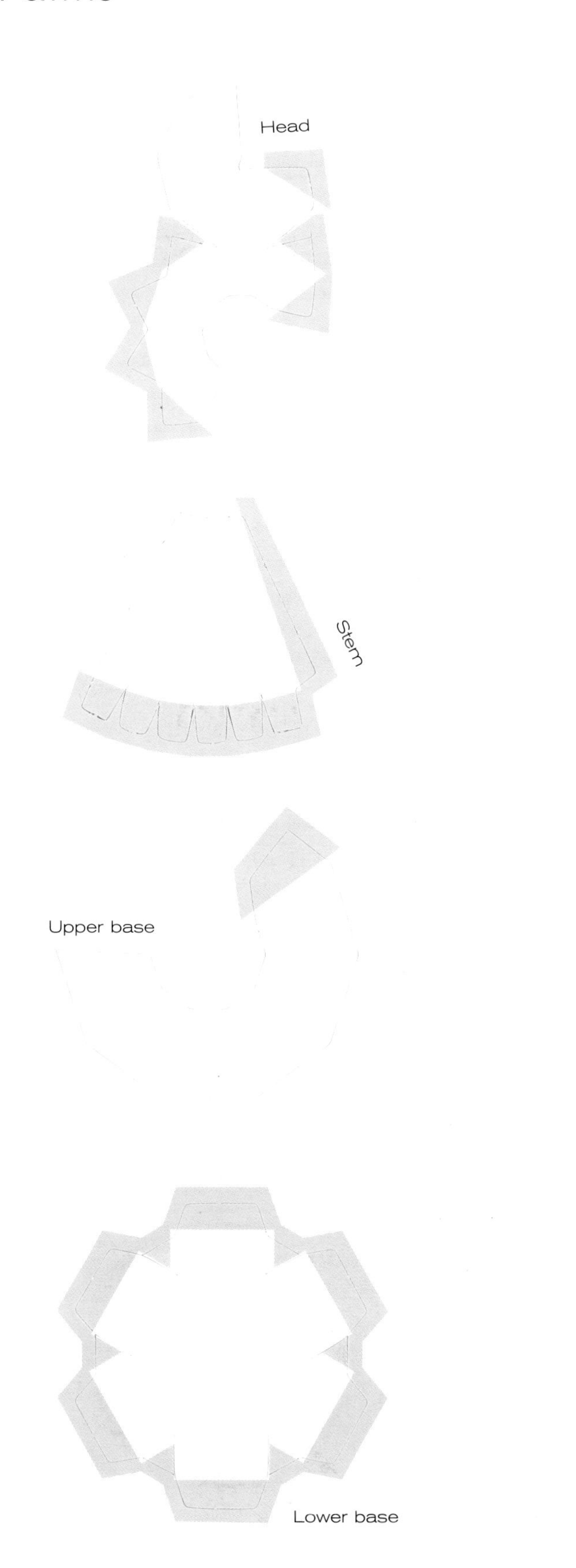

White Pawn 5

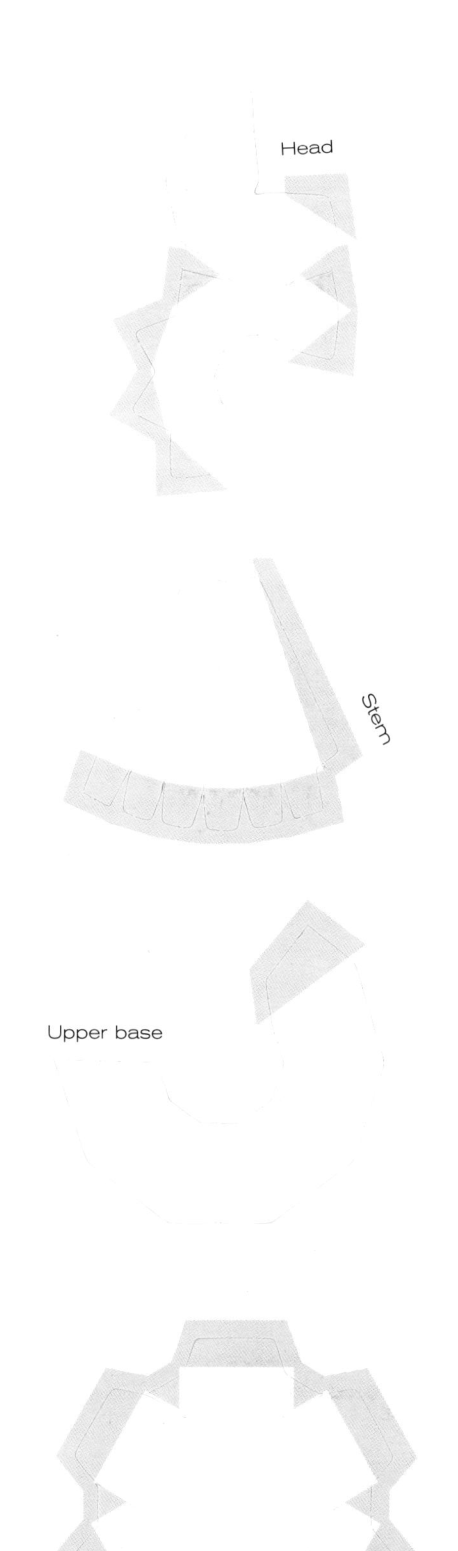

White Pawn 6

The White Pawns

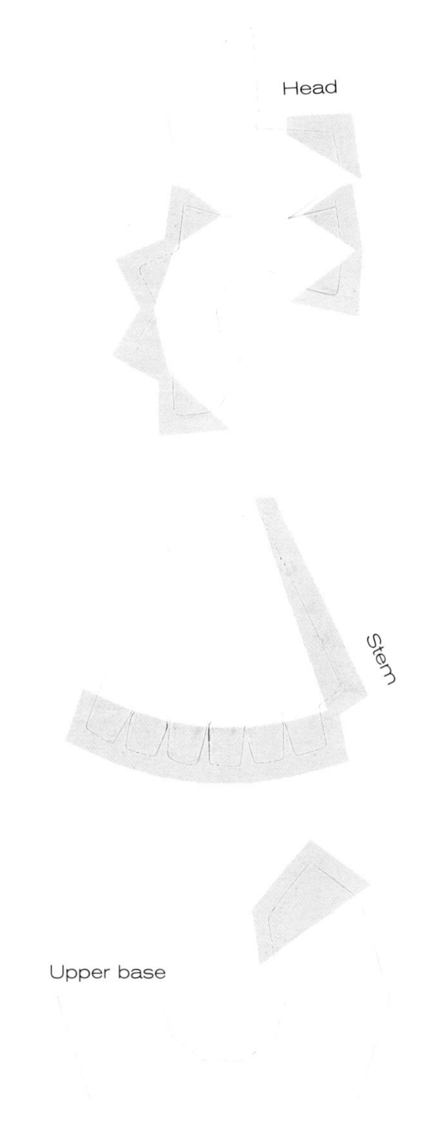

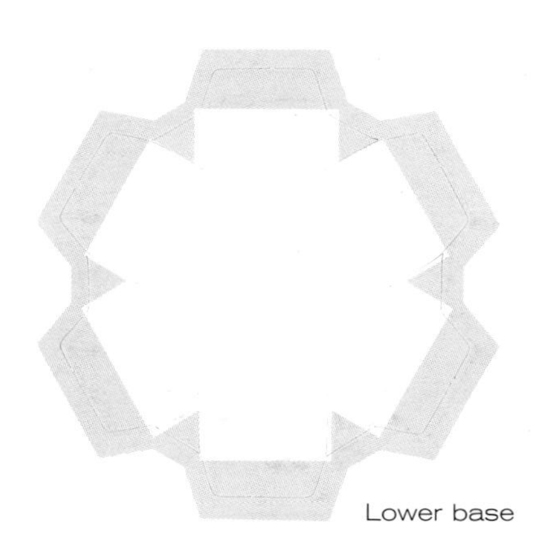

White Pawn 7

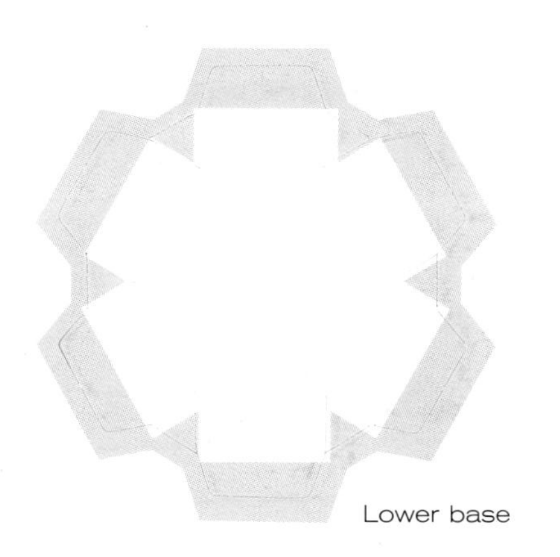

White Pawn 8

The White Bishops

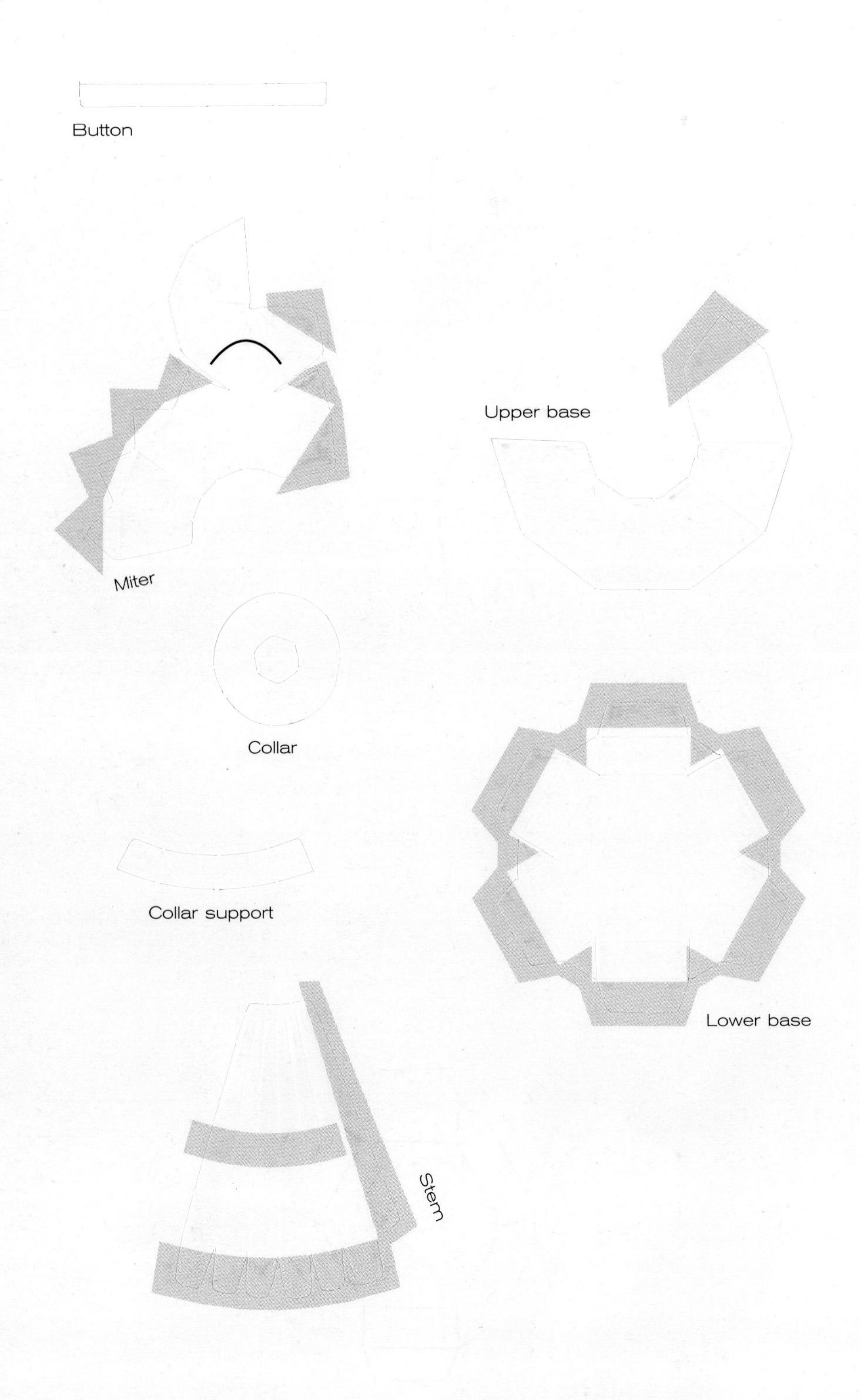

White Bishop 1

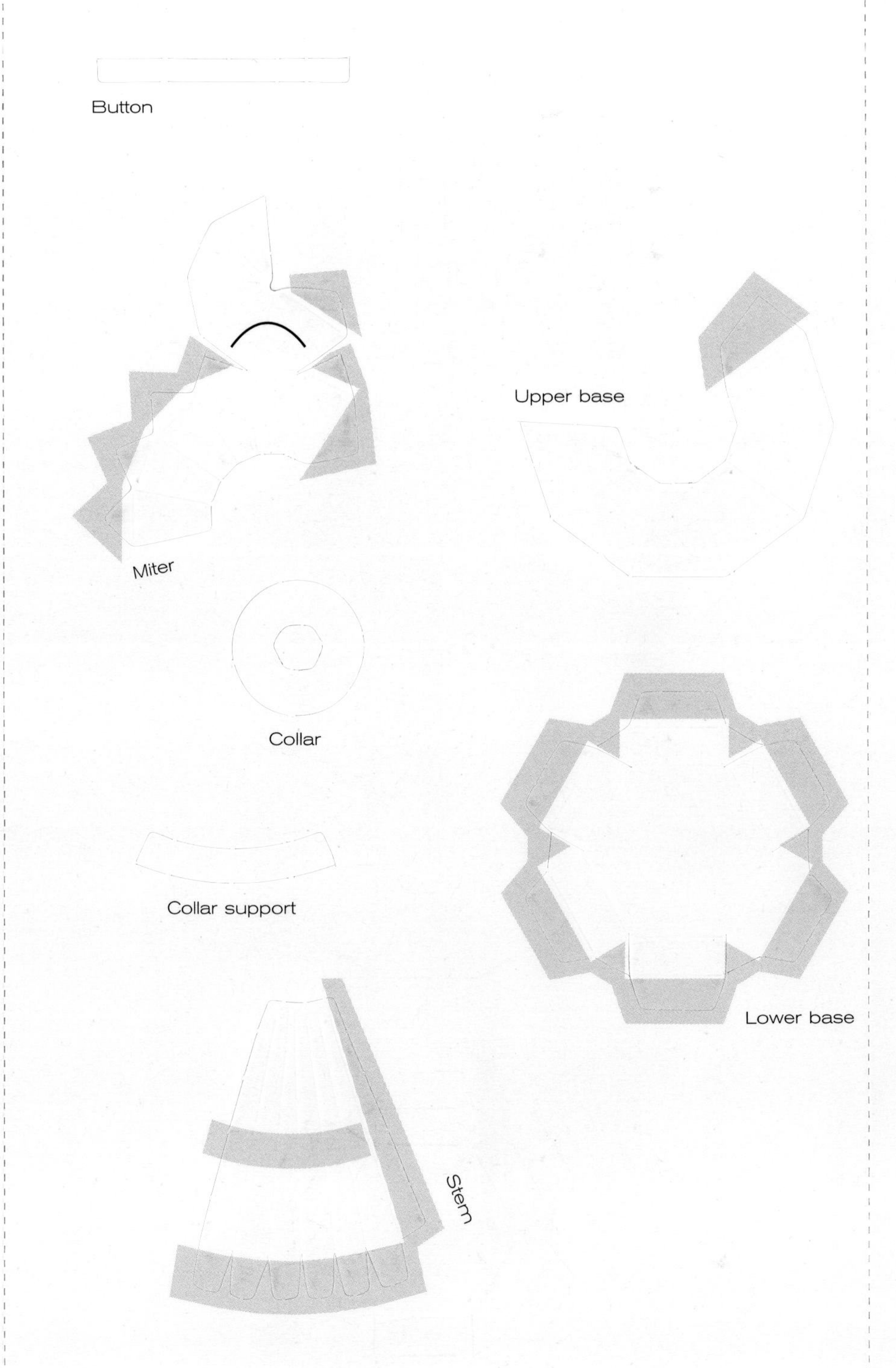

White Bishop 2

The White Knights

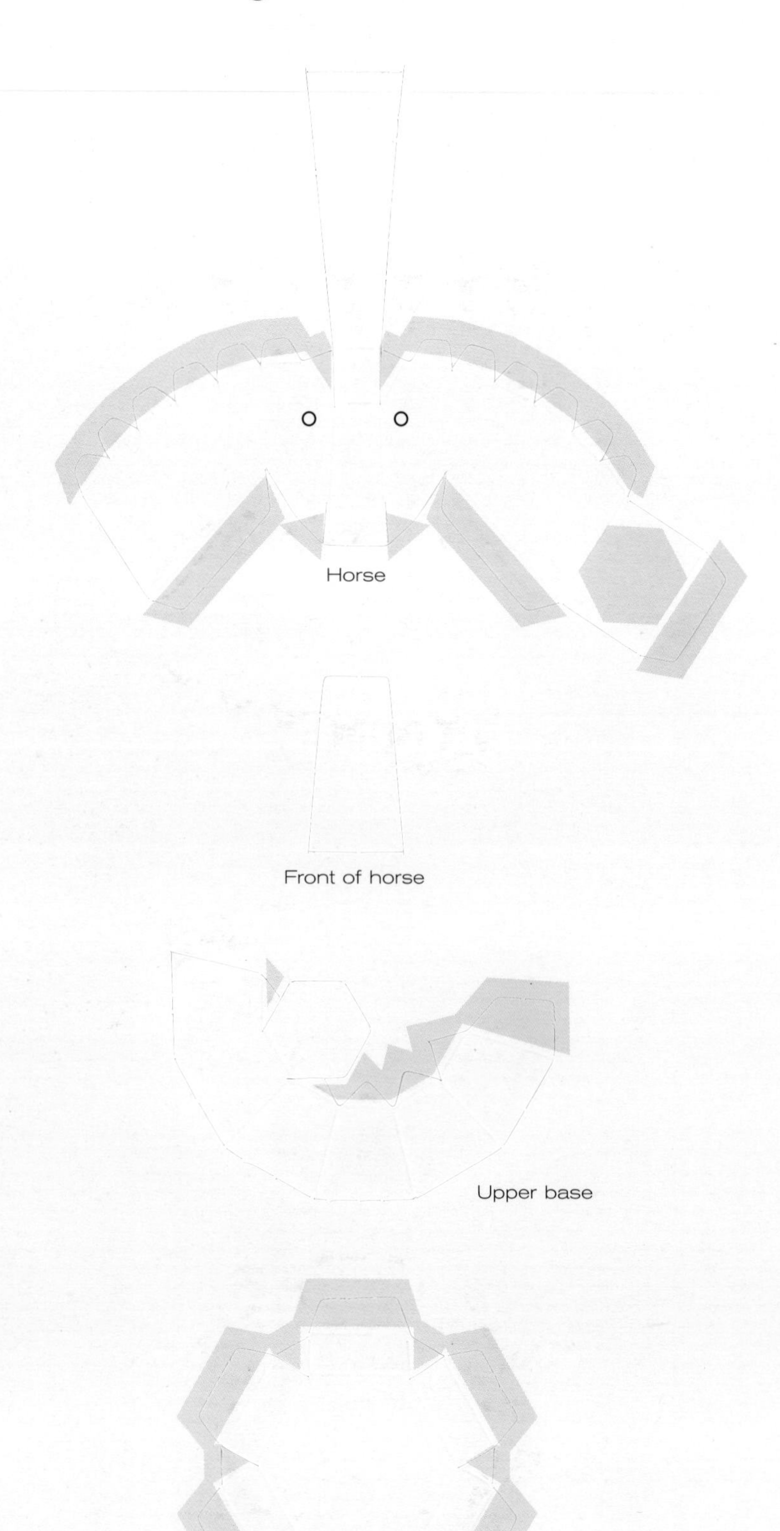

White Knight 1

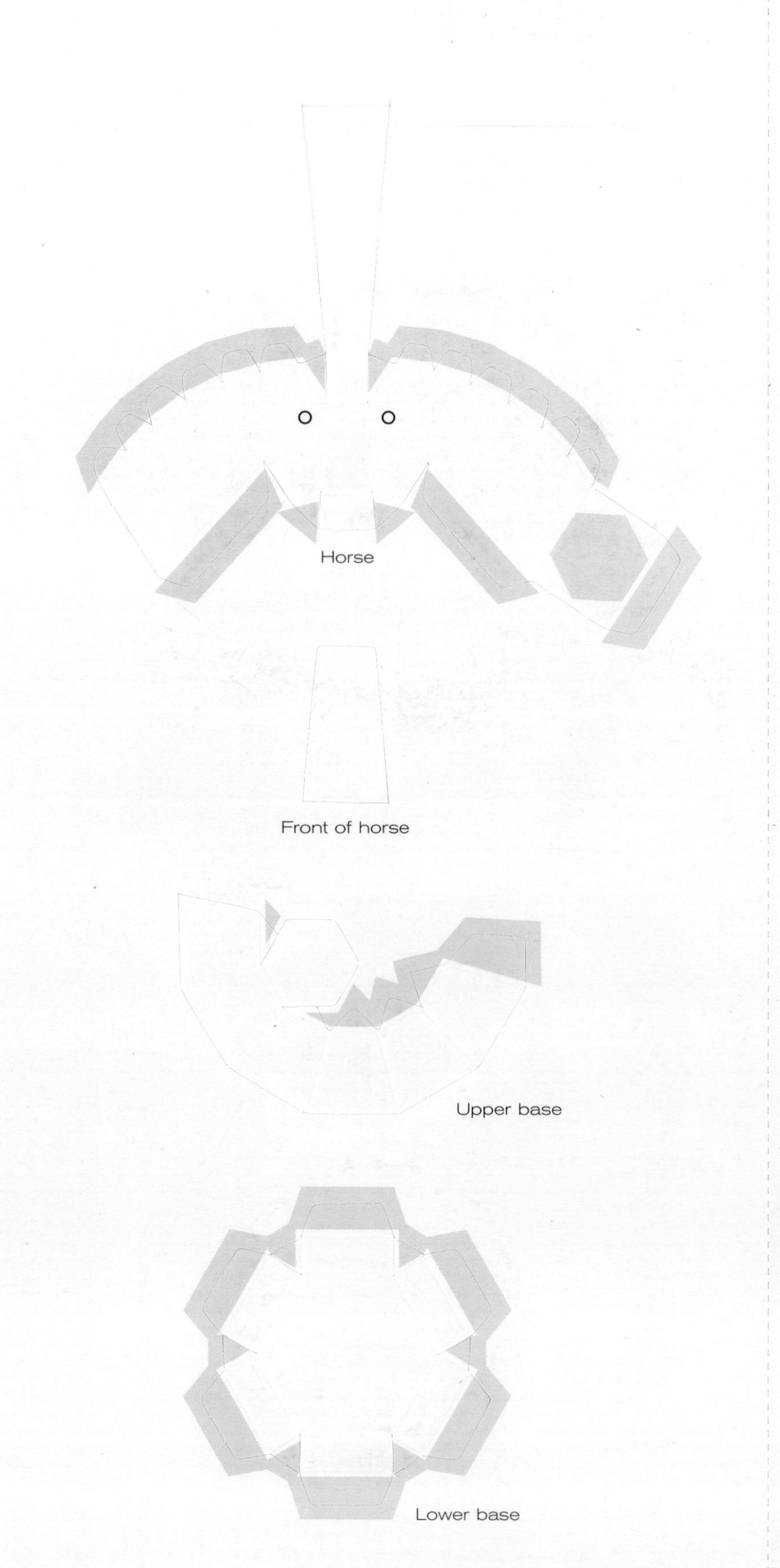

White Knight 2

The White Rooks

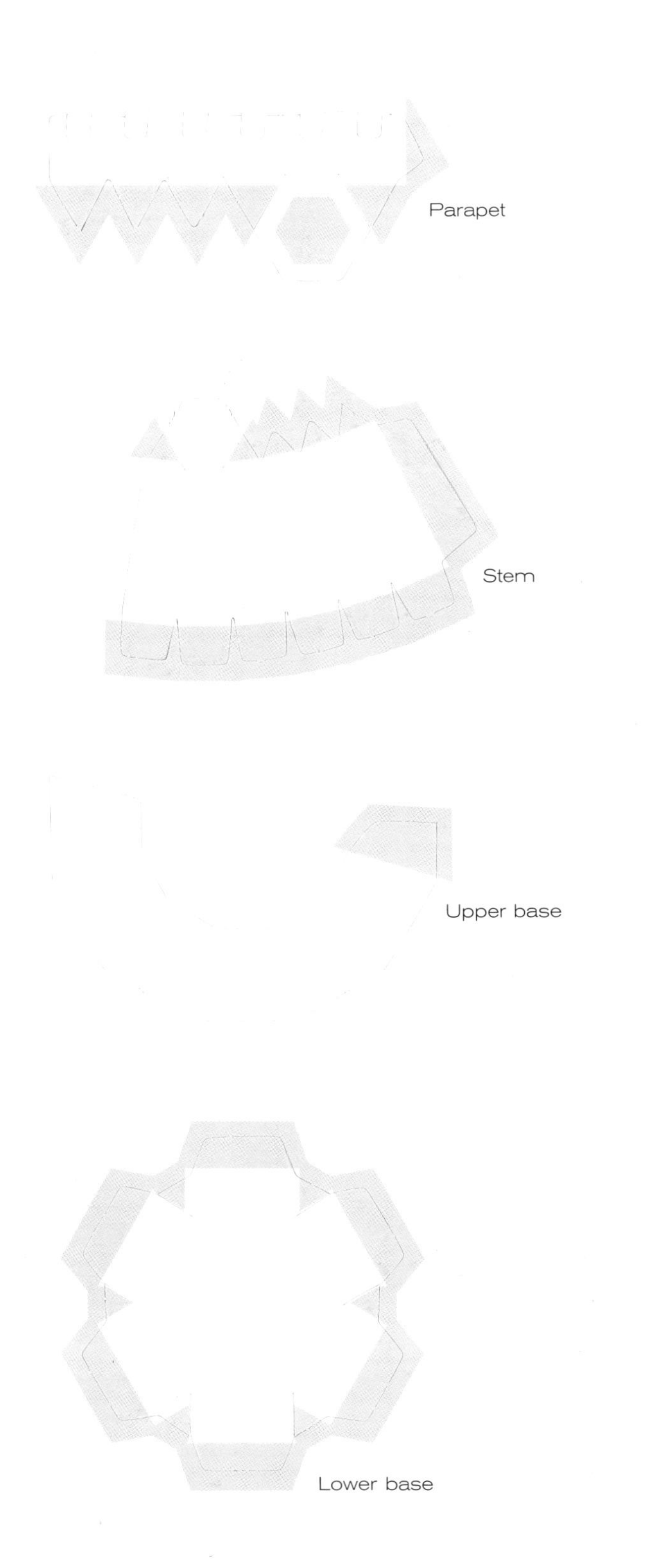

White Rook 1

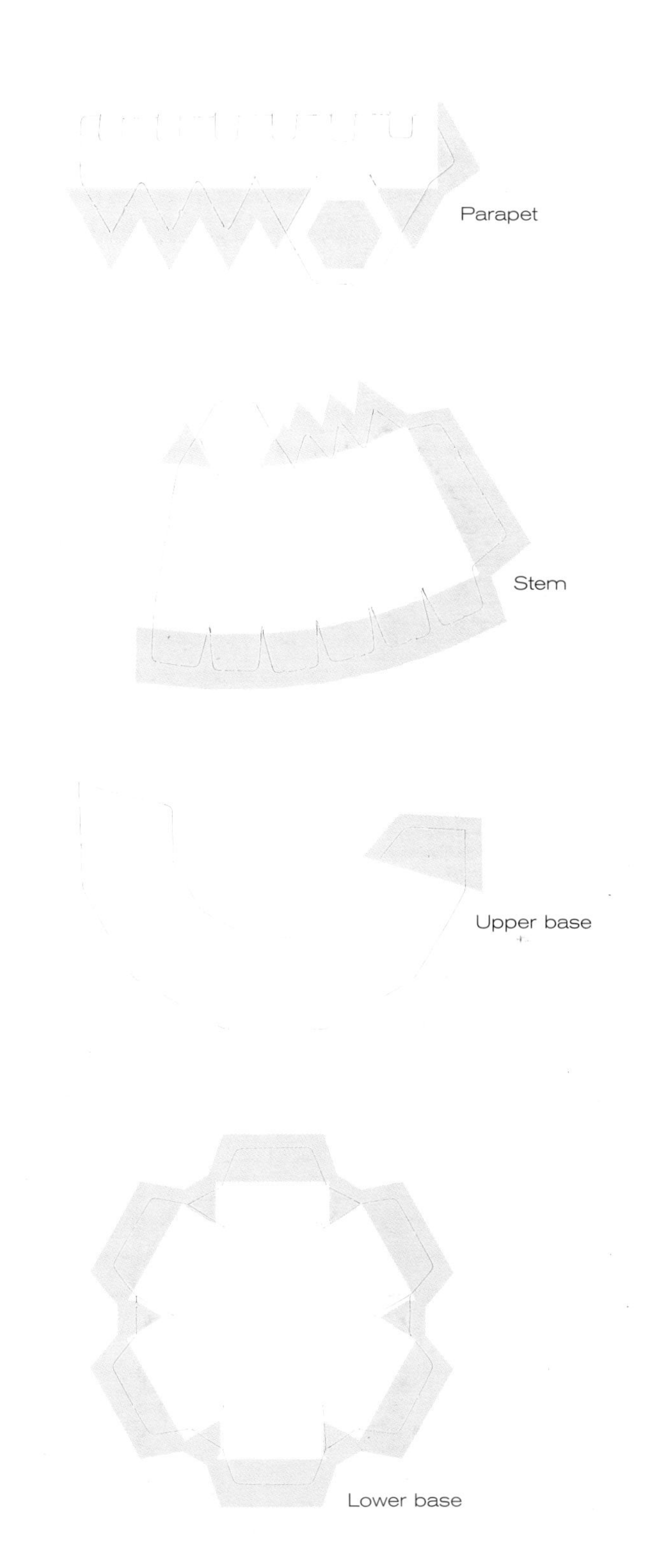

White Rook 2

The White Queen & King

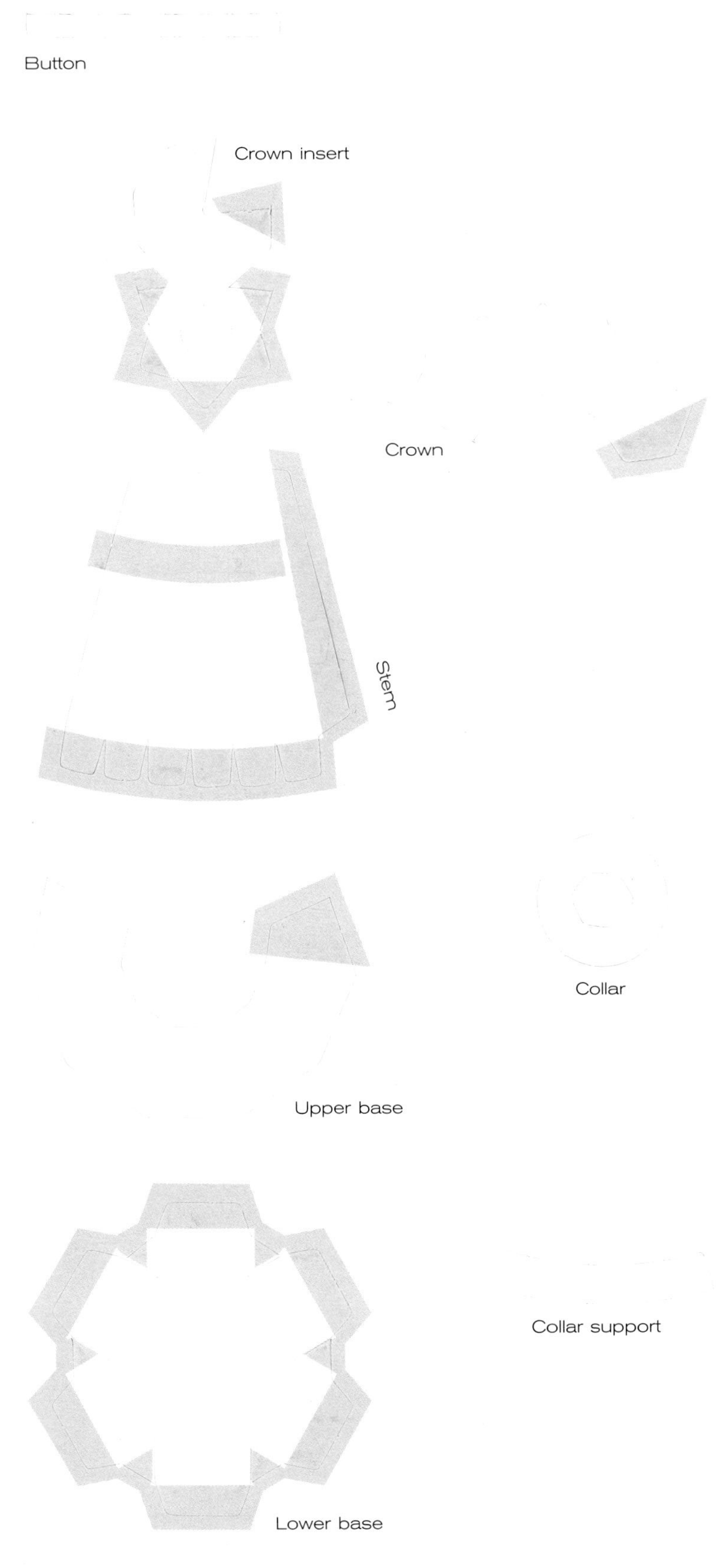

White Queen

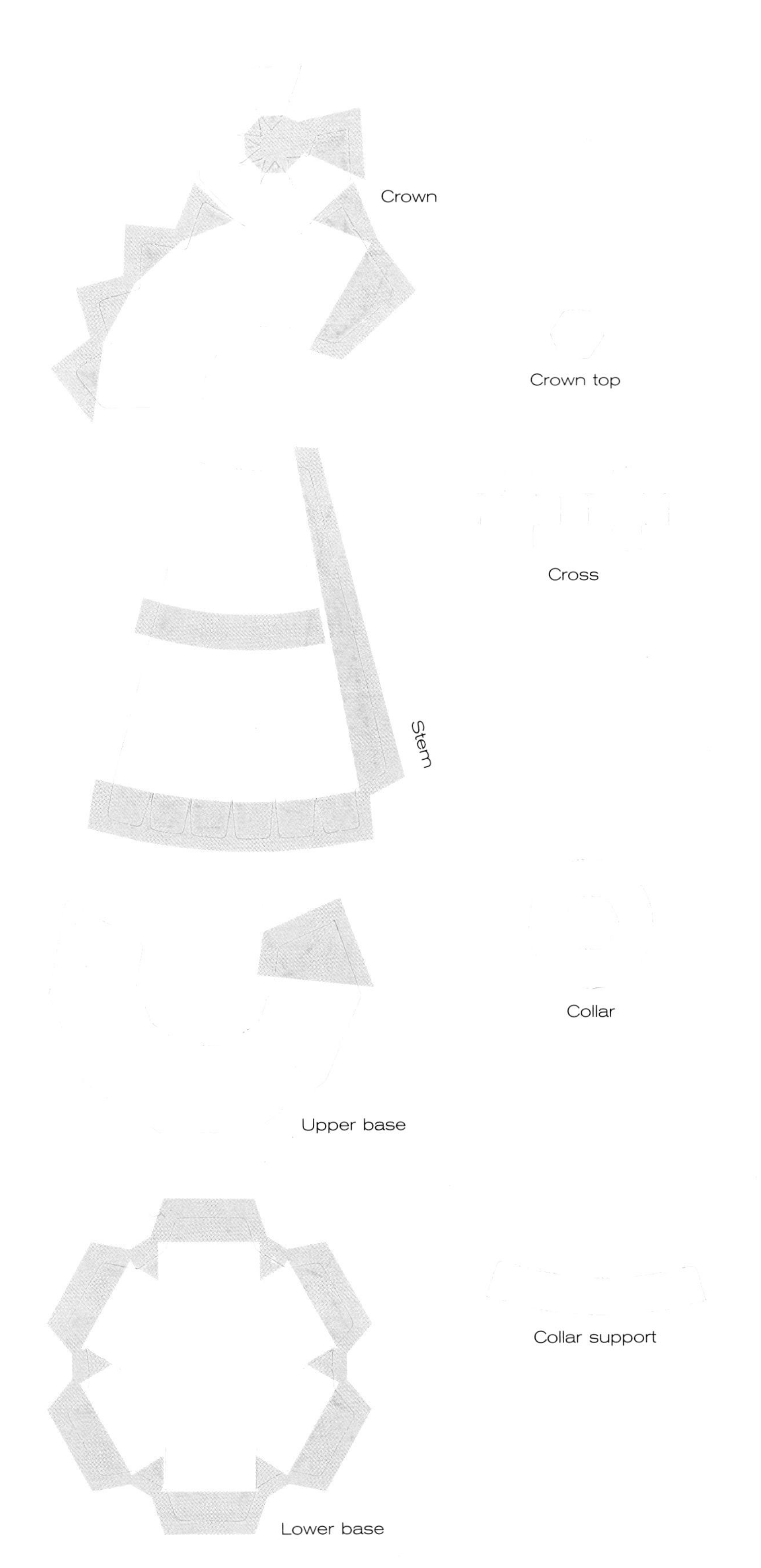

White King

The Black Pawns

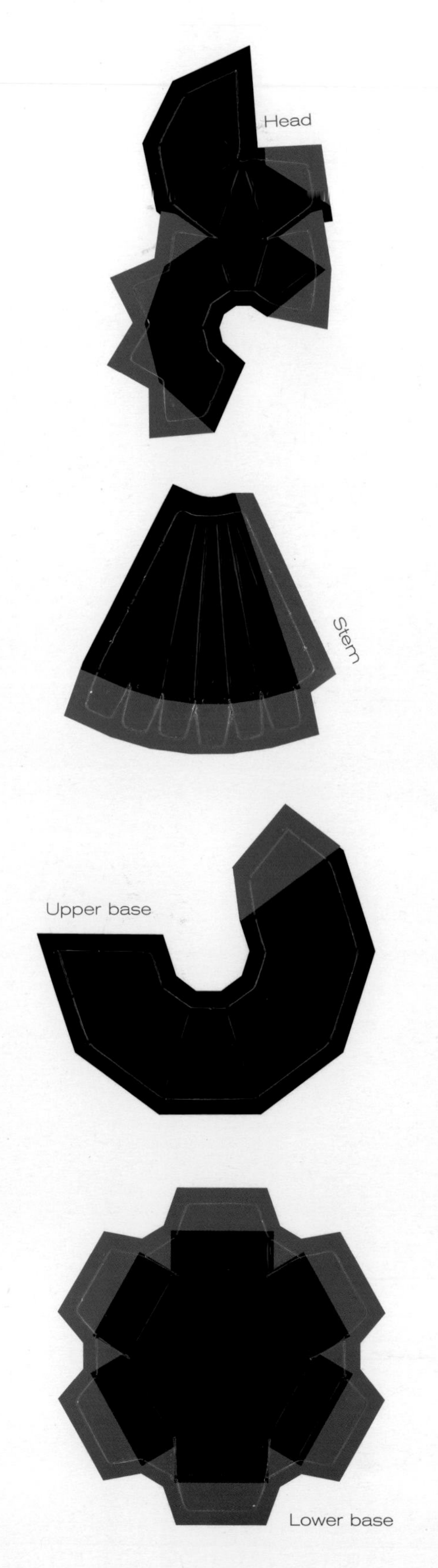

Black Pawn 1

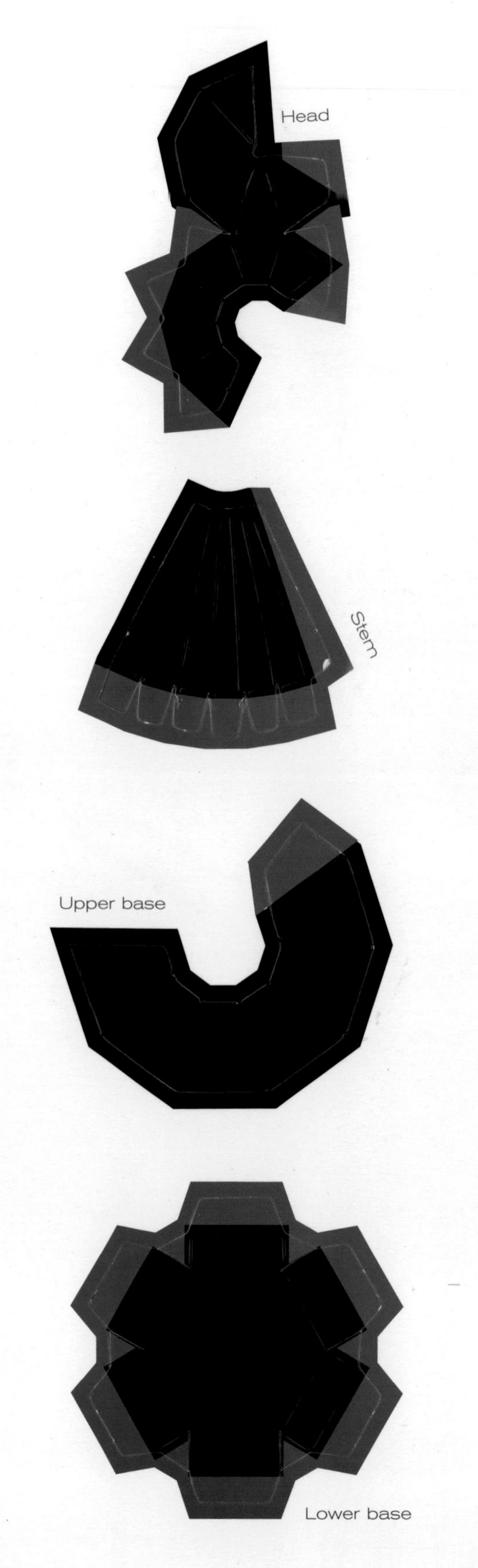

Black Pawn 2

The Black Pawns

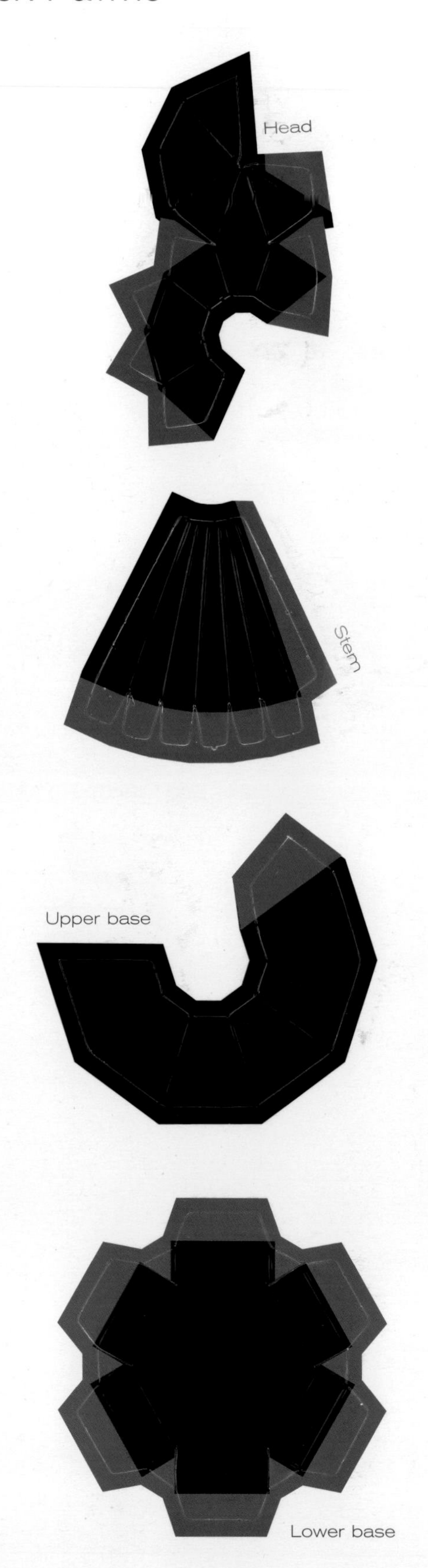

Black Pawn 3

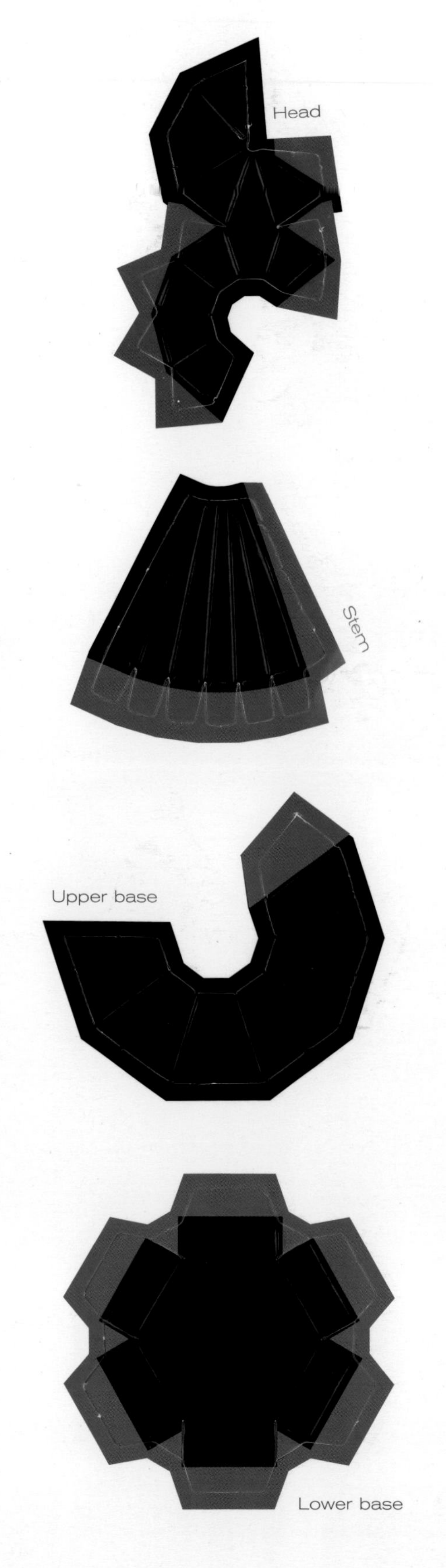

Black Pawn 4

The Black Pawns

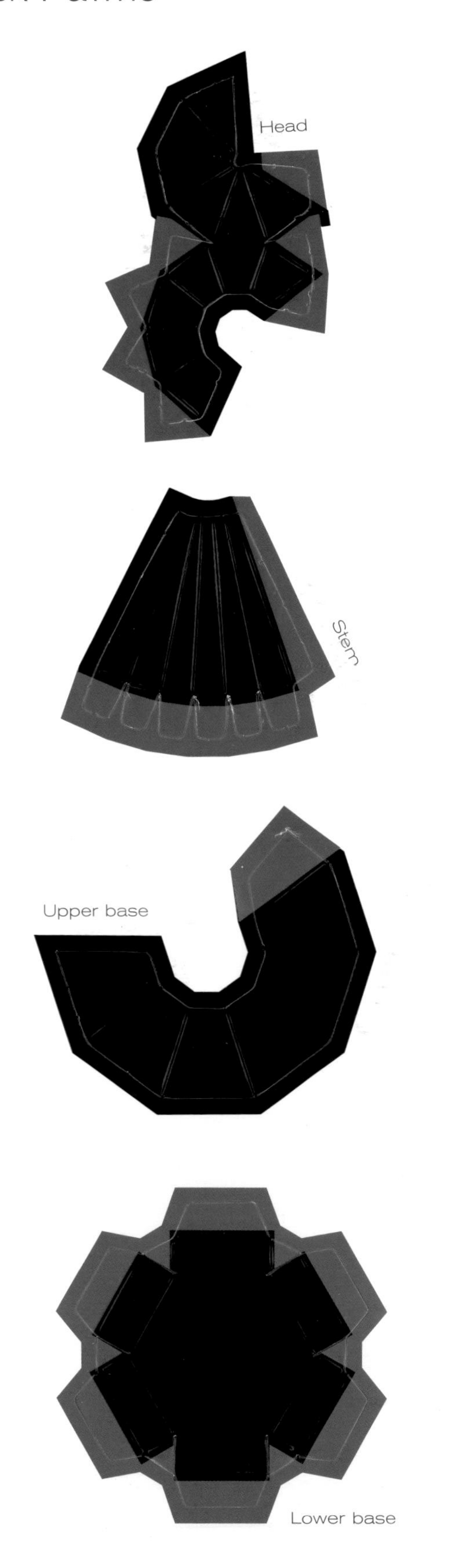

Black Pawn 5

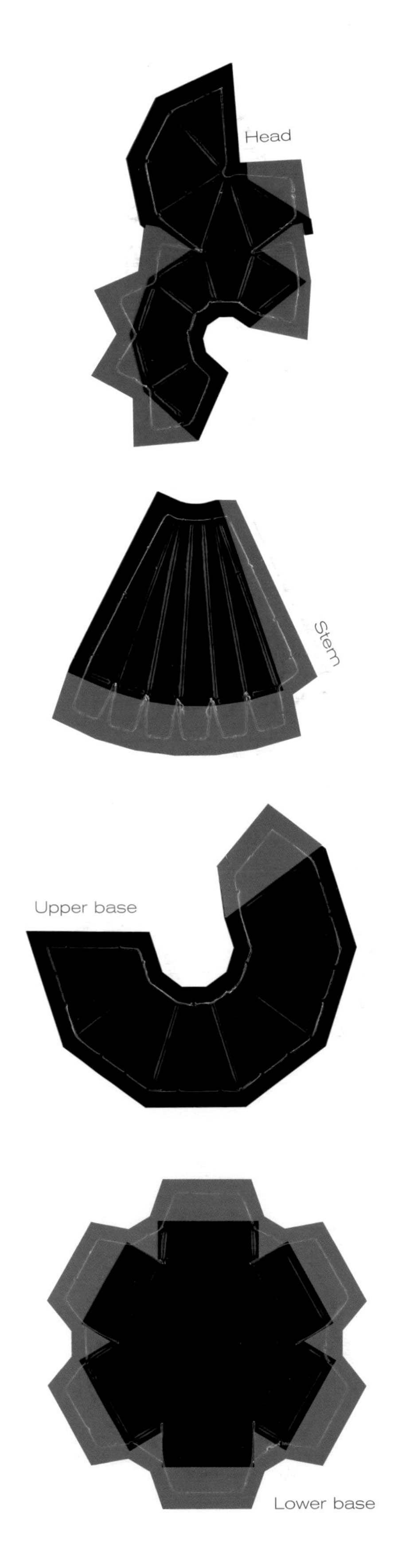

Black Pawn 6

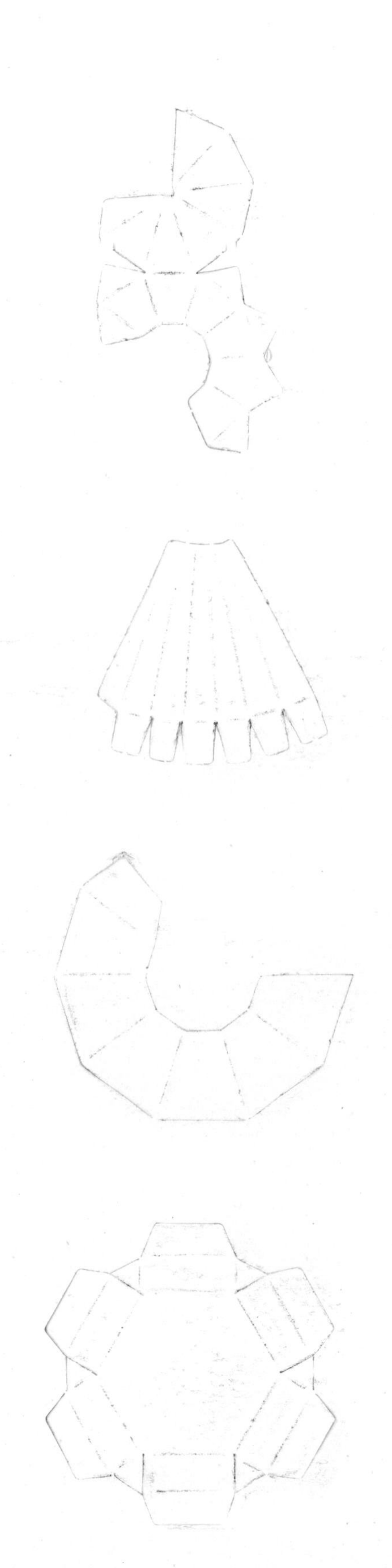

The Black Pawns

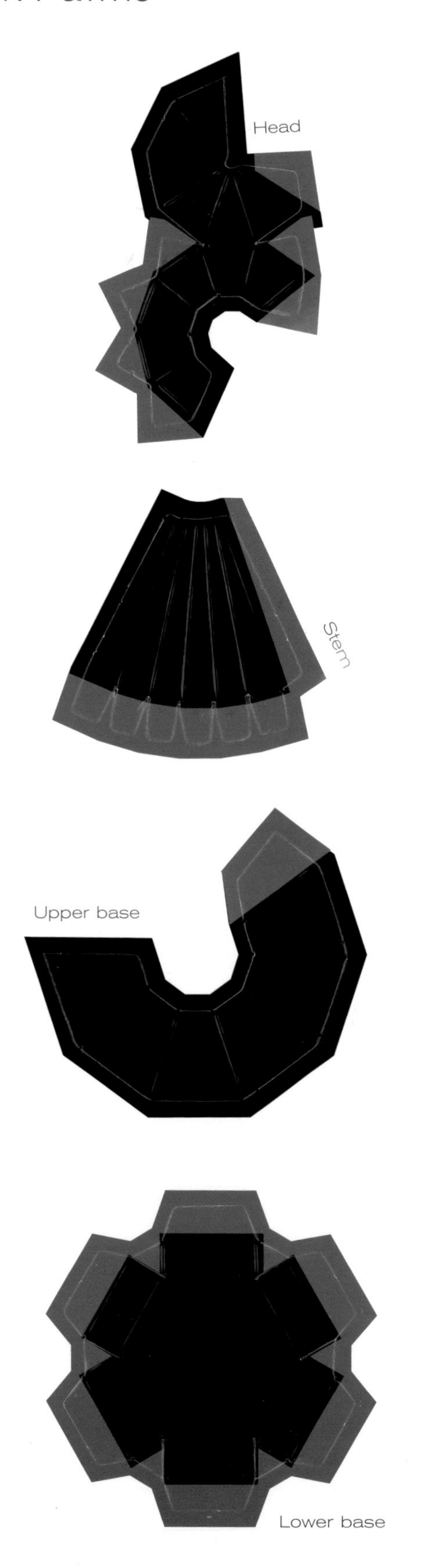

Black Pawn 7

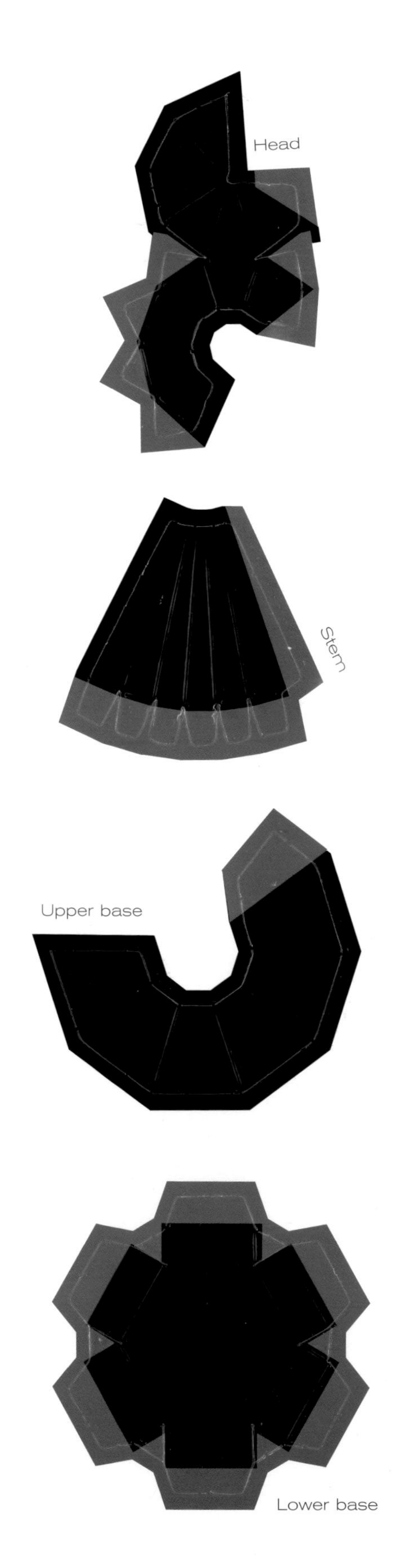

Black Pawn 8

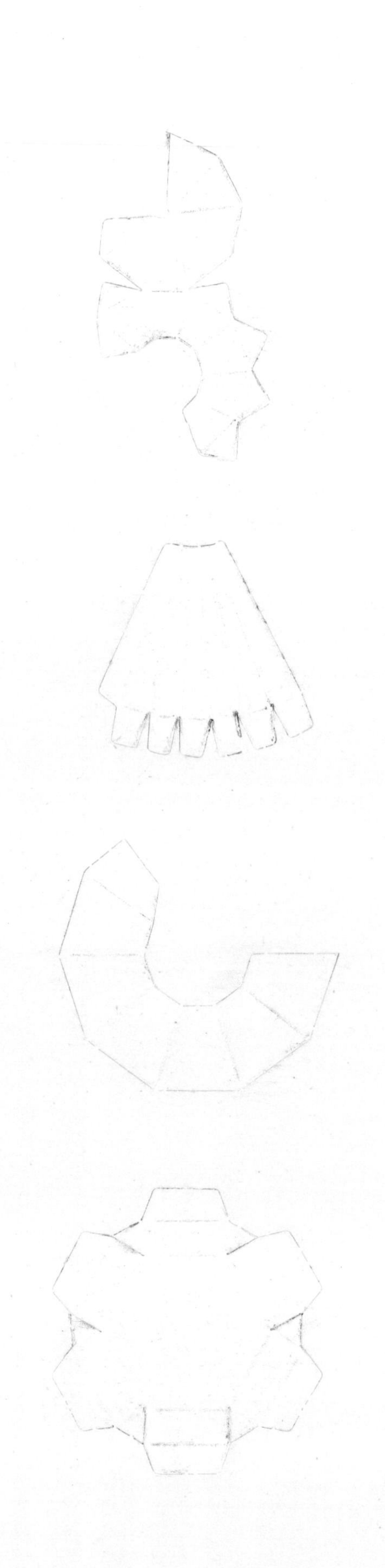
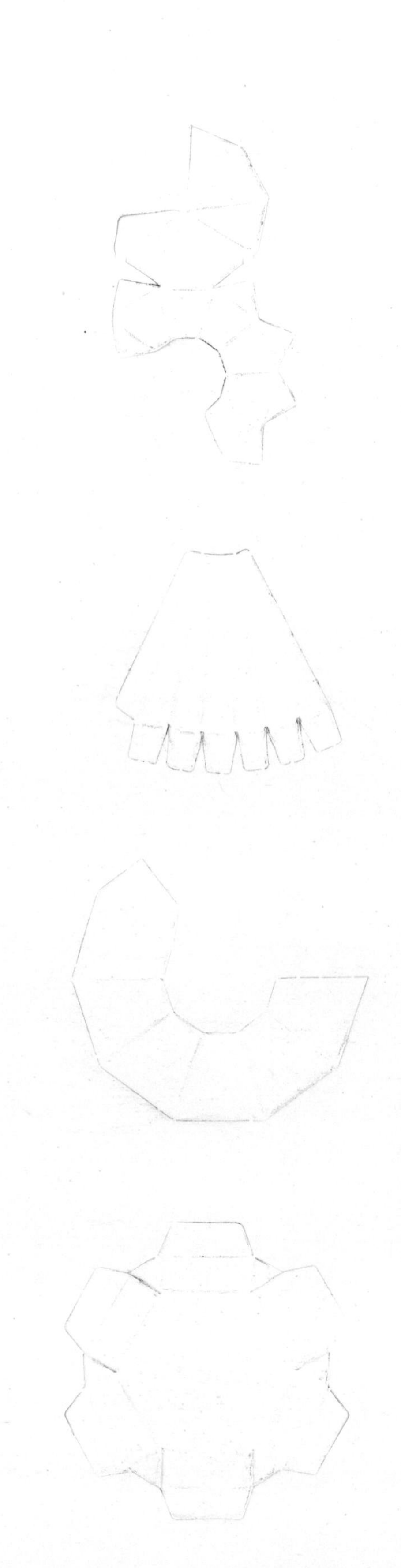

The Black Bishops

Black Bishop 1

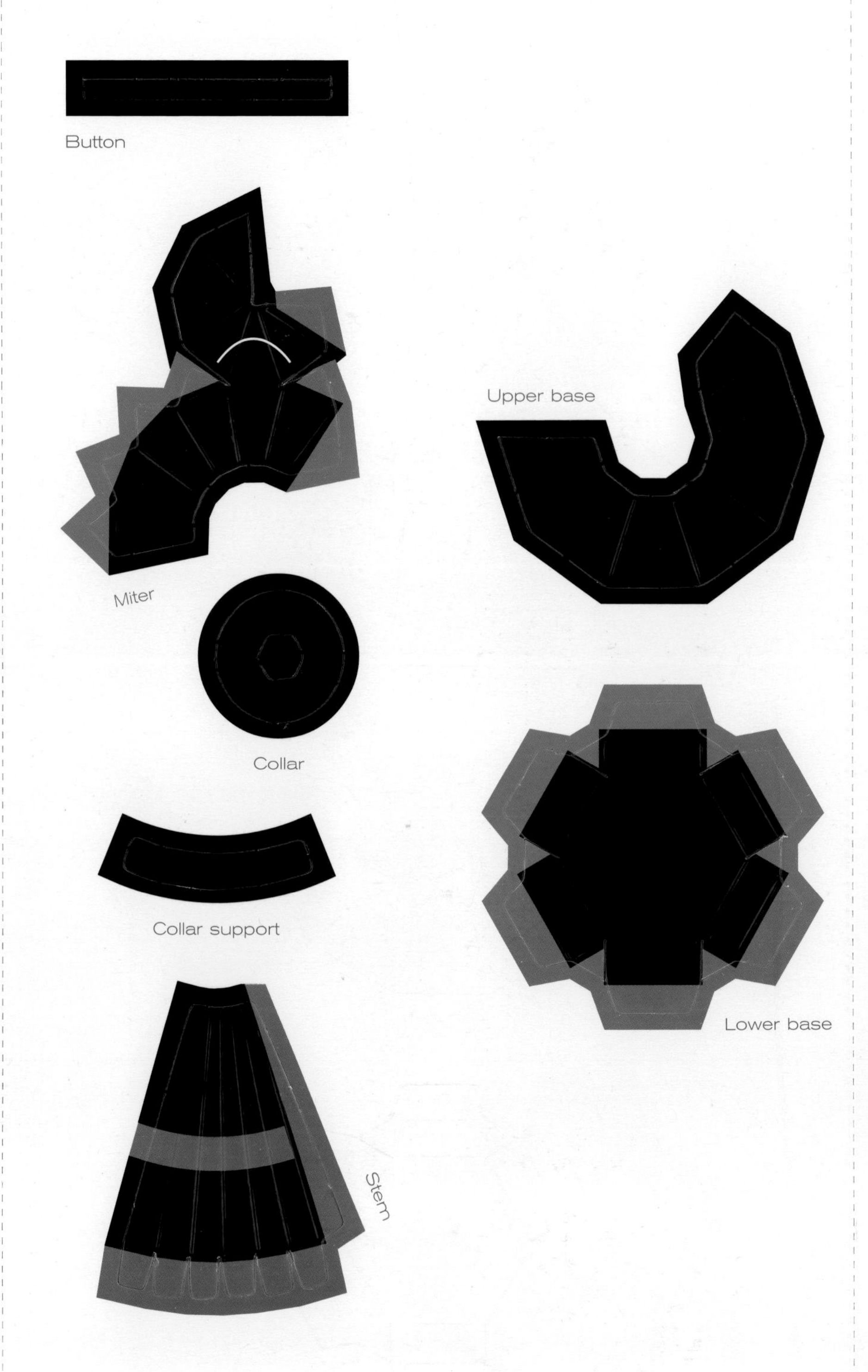

Black Bishop 2

The Black Knights

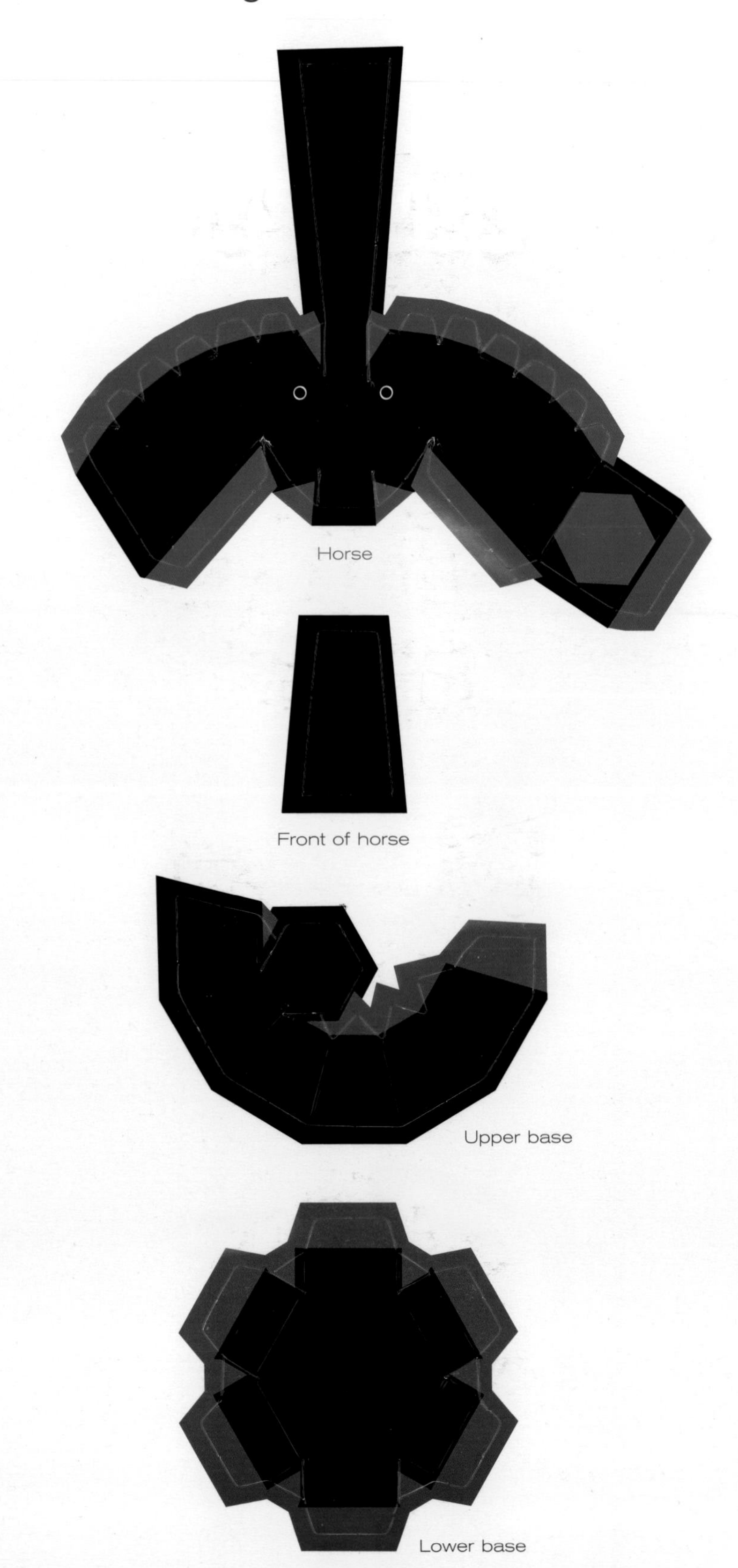

Black Knight 1

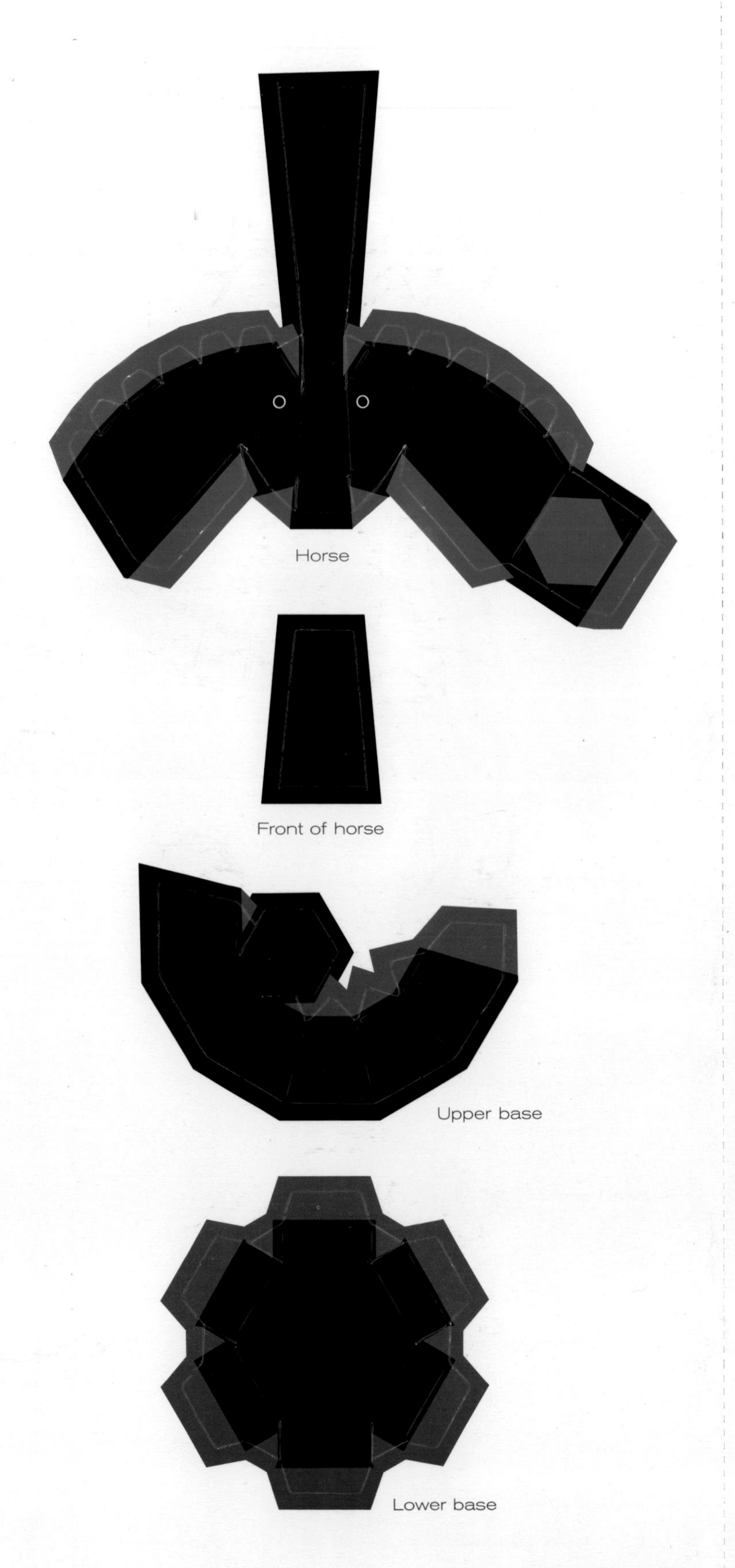

Black Knight 2

The Black Rooks

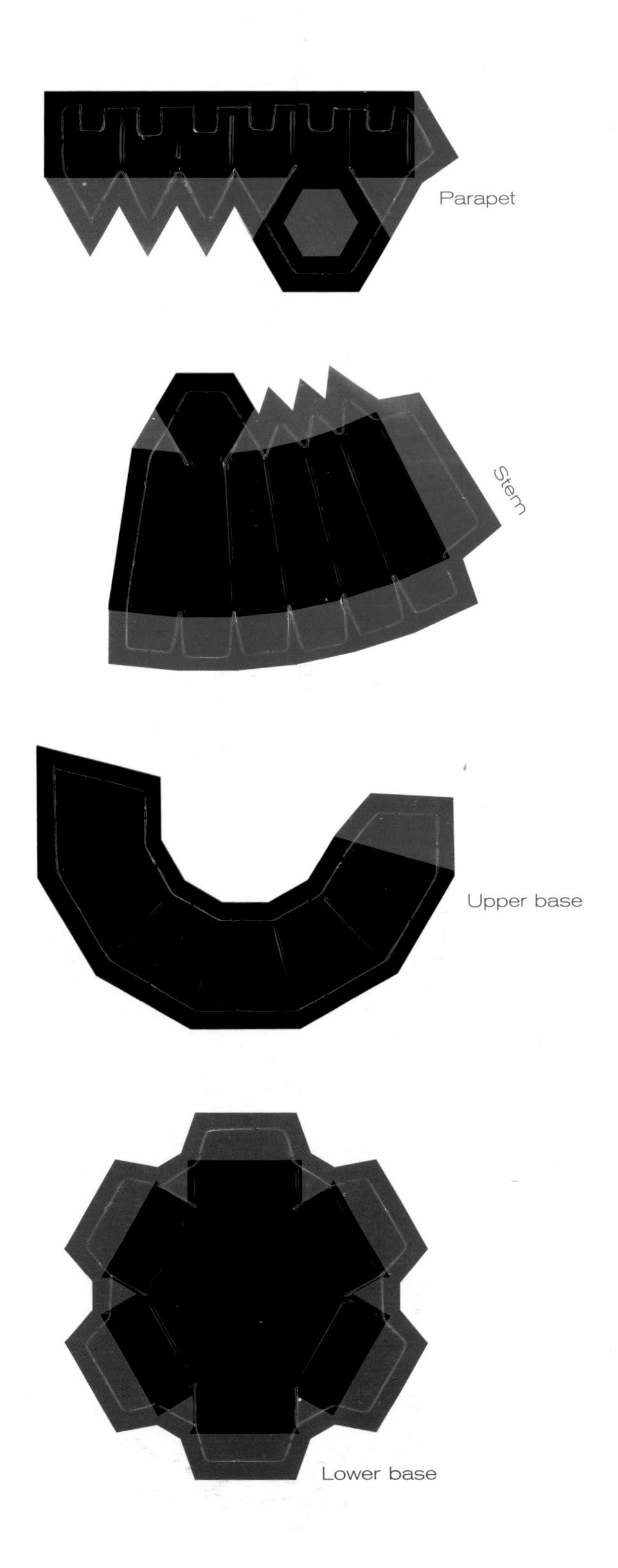

Black Rook 1

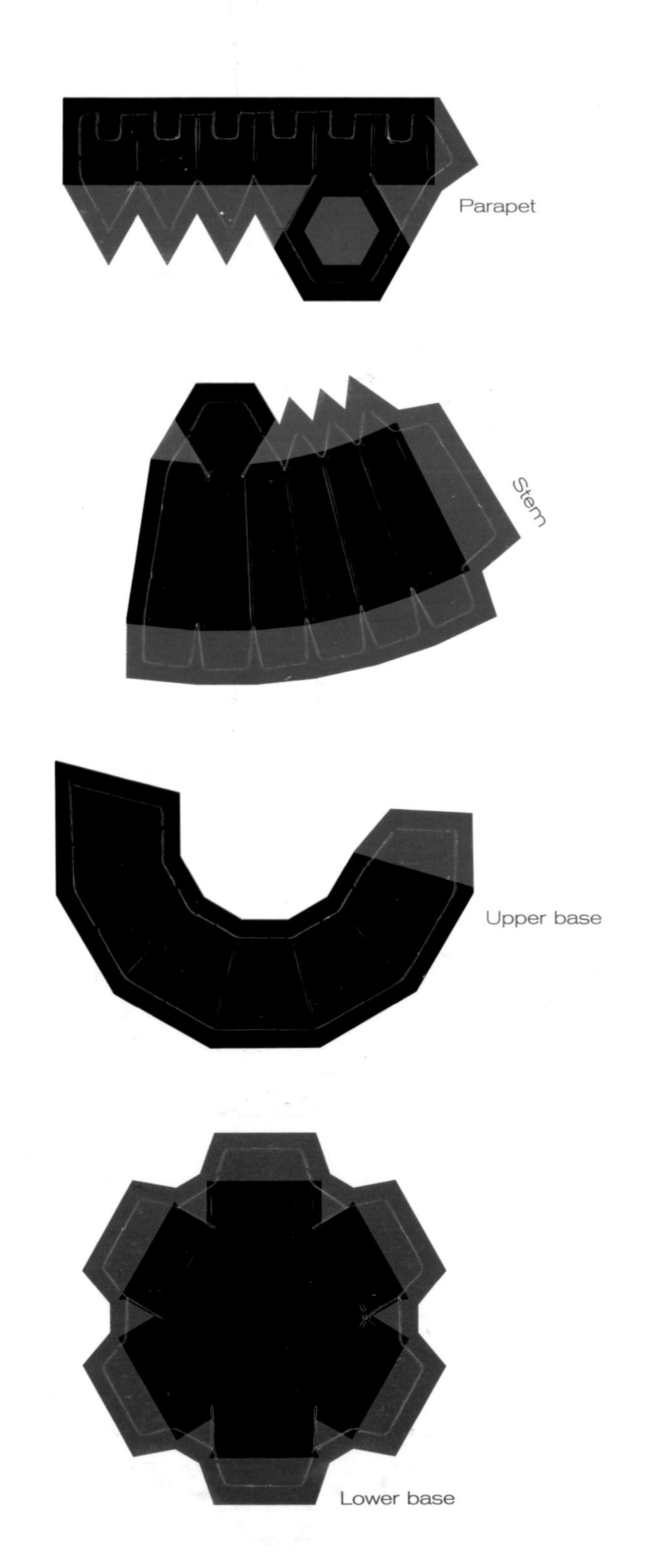

Black Rook 2

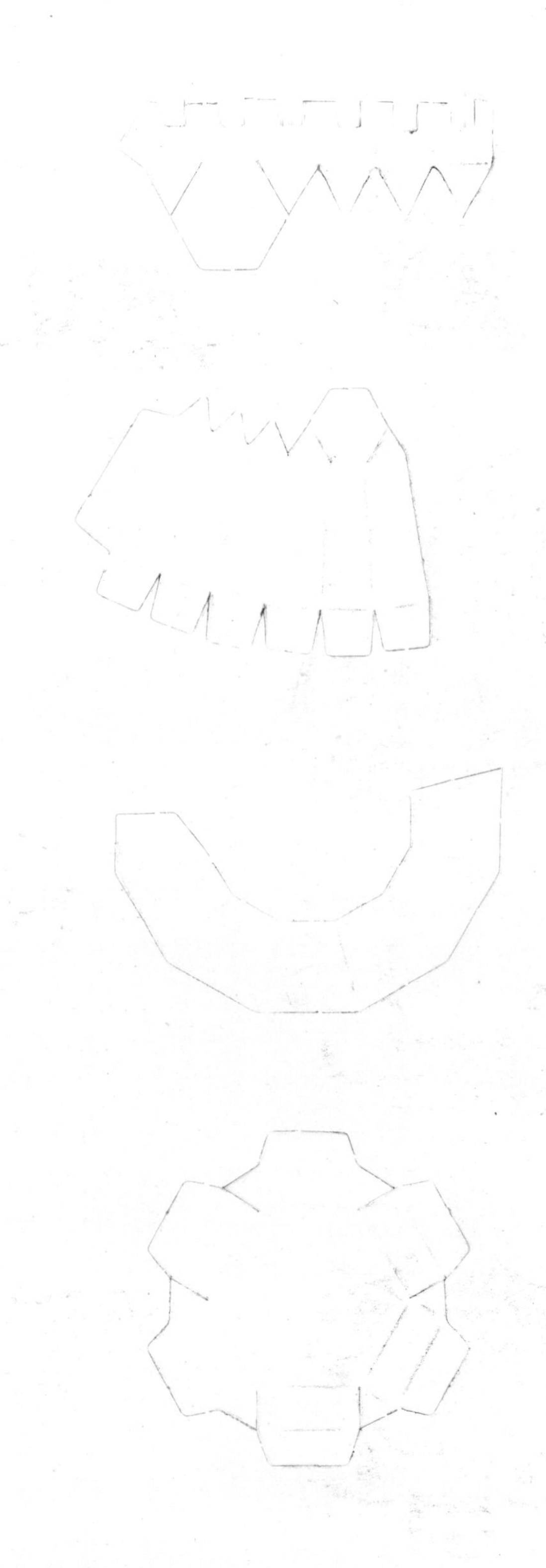

The Black Queen & King

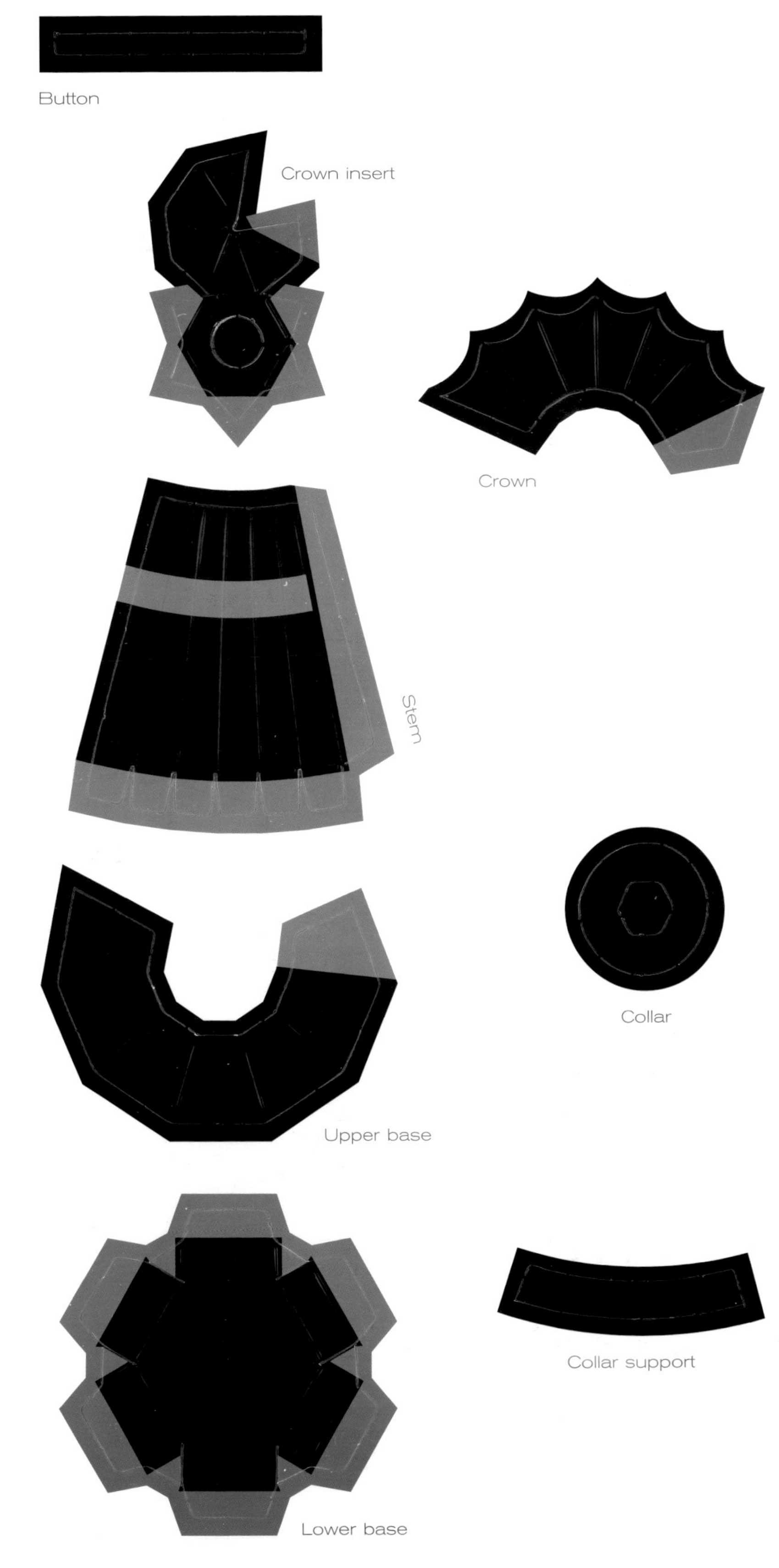

Black Queen

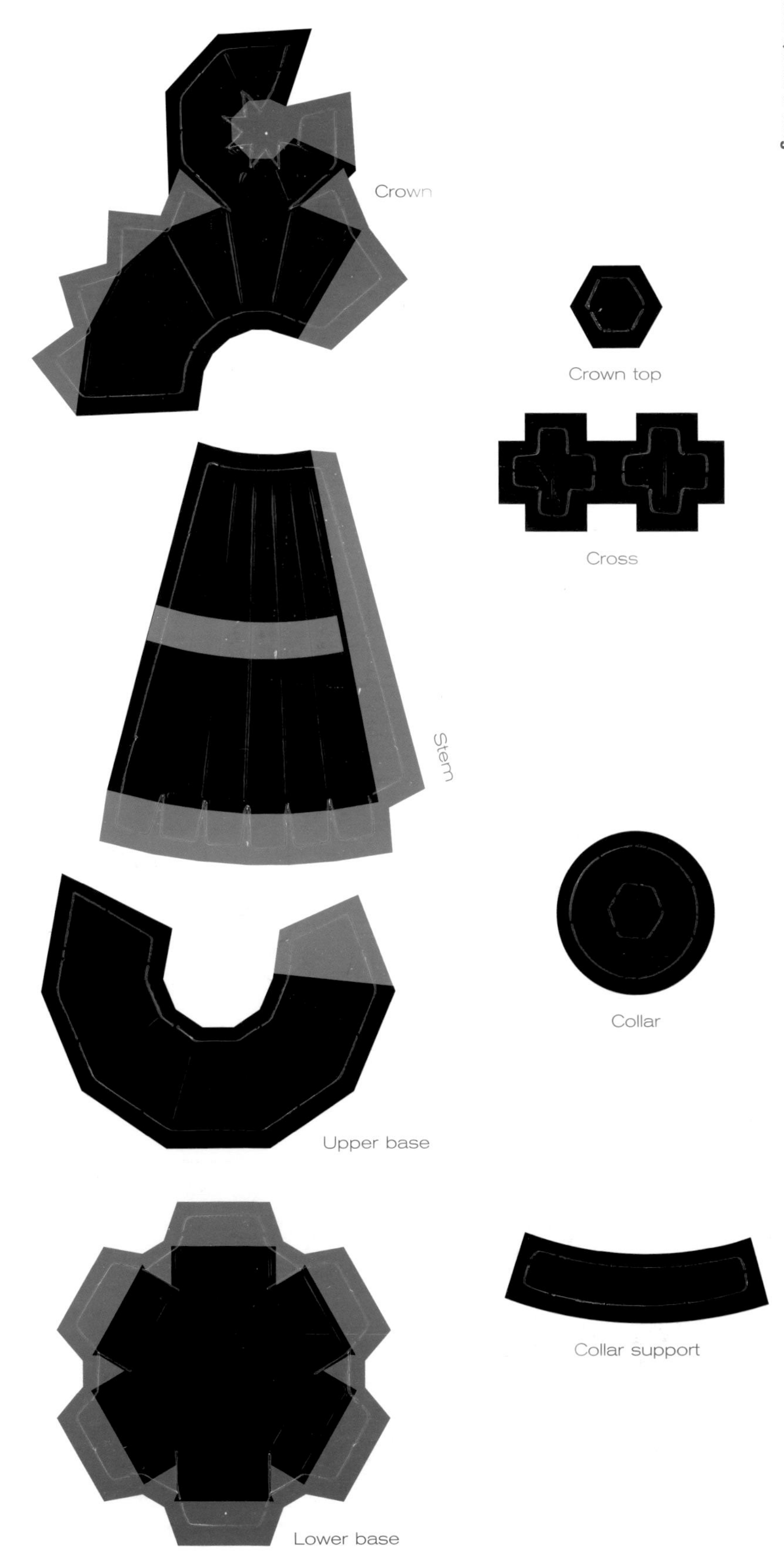

Black King

The White Pawns (second set)

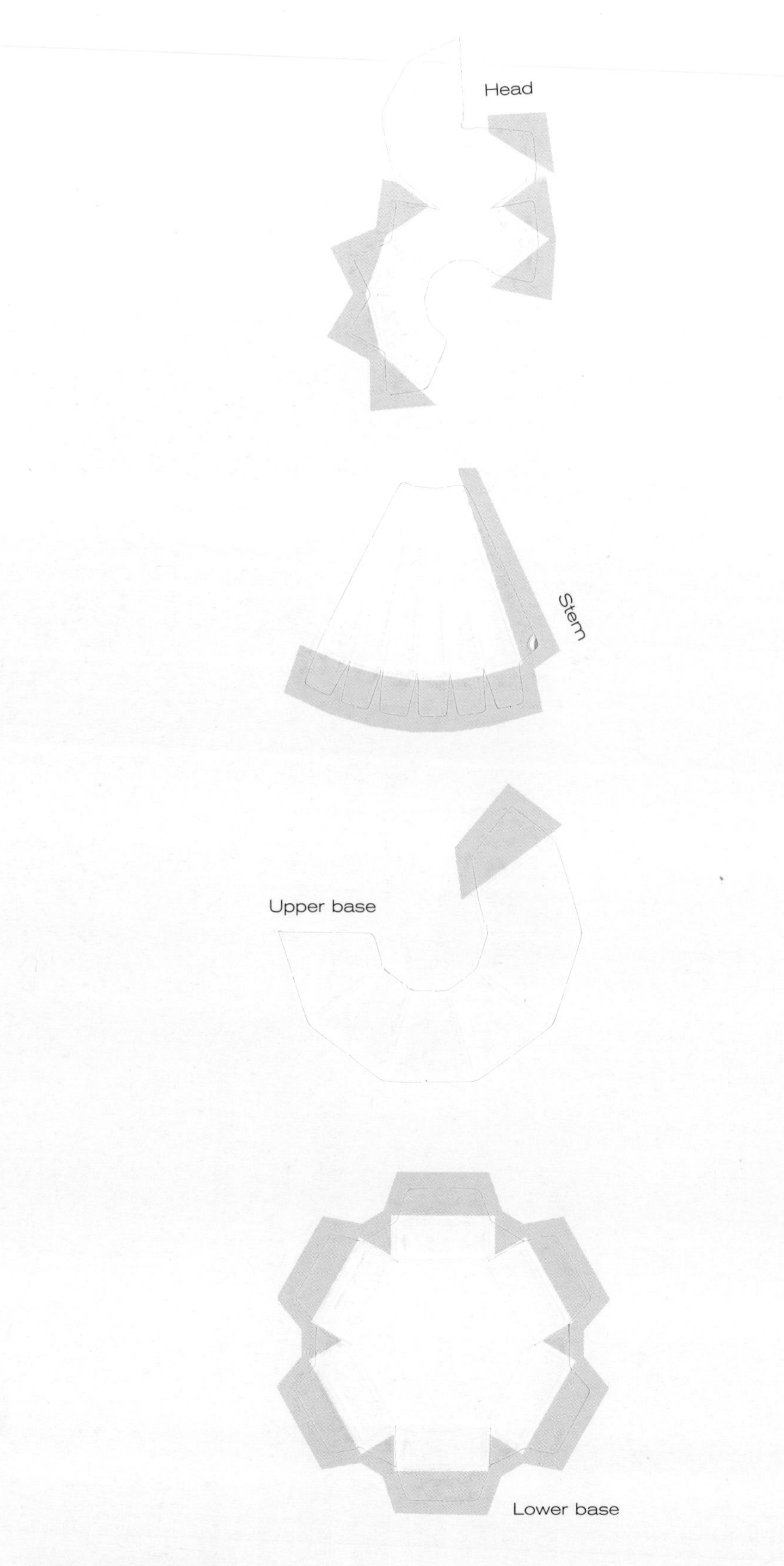

Spare White Pawn 1

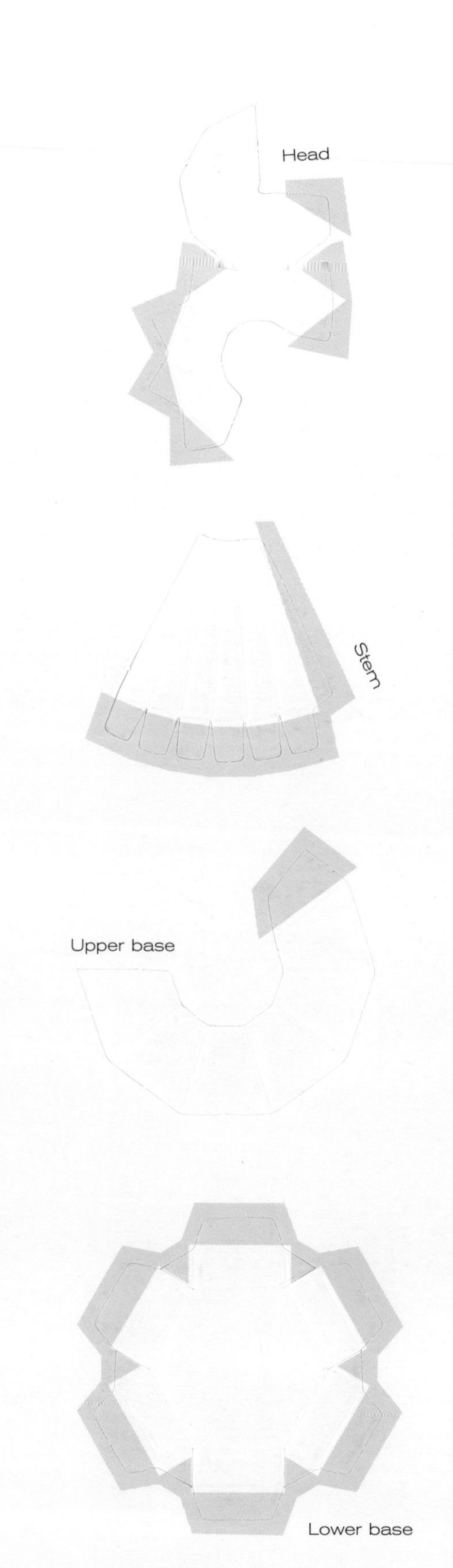

Spare White Pawn 2

The White Pawns (second set)

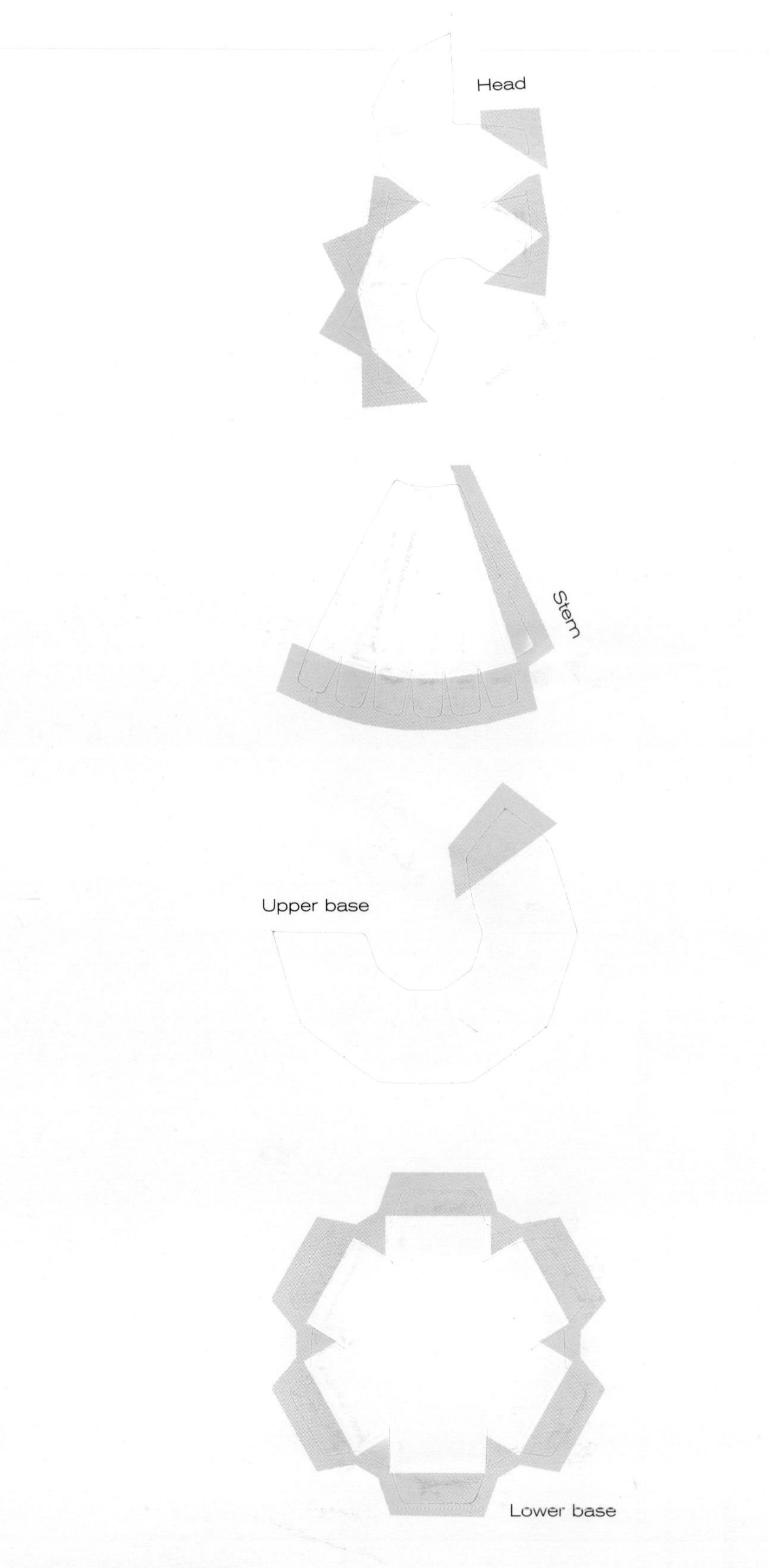

Spare White Pawn 3

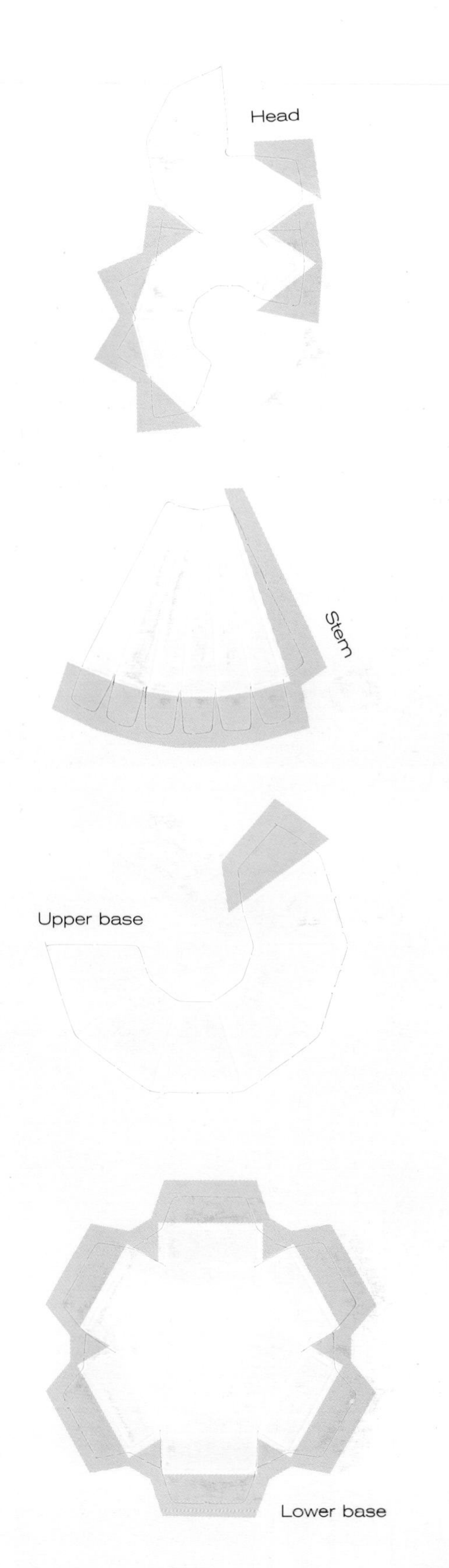

Spare White Pawn 4

The White Pawns (second set)

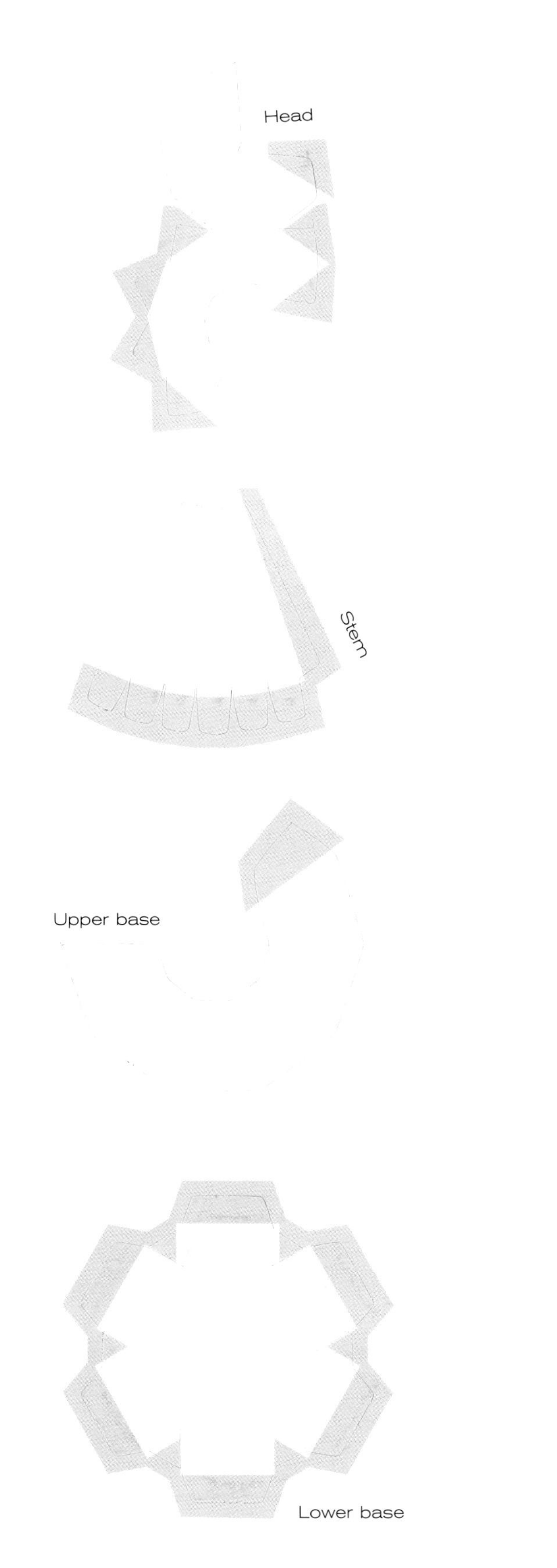

Spare White Pawn 5

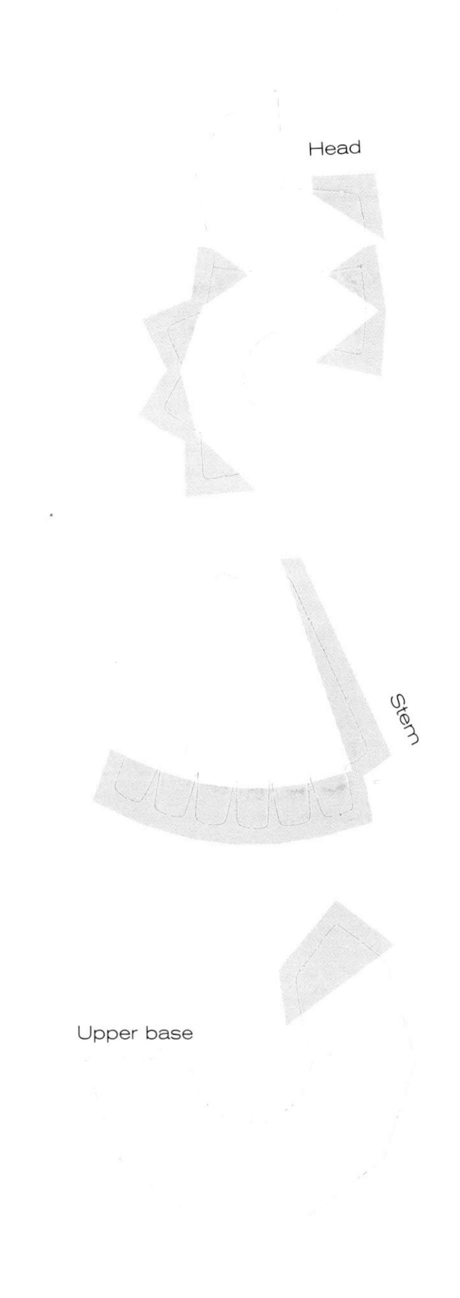

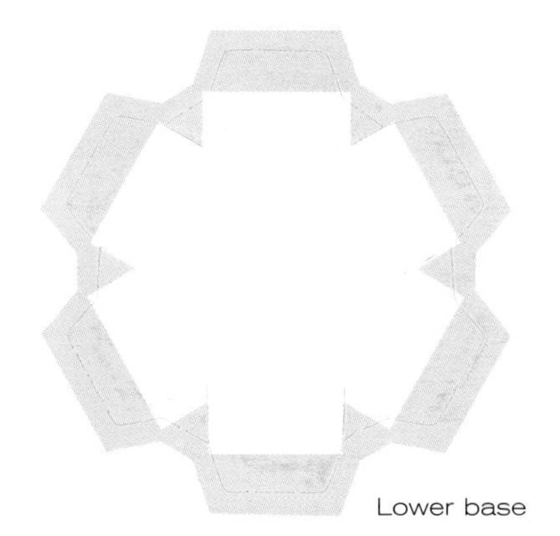

Spare White Pawn 6

The White Pawns (second set)

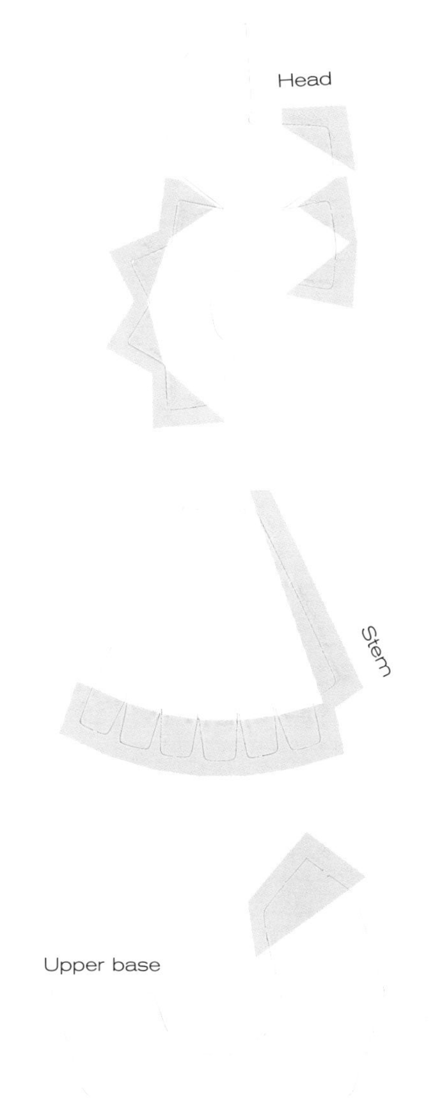

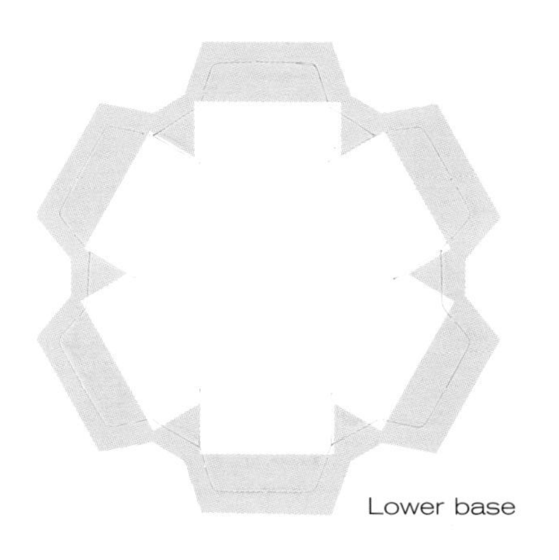

Spare White Pawn 7

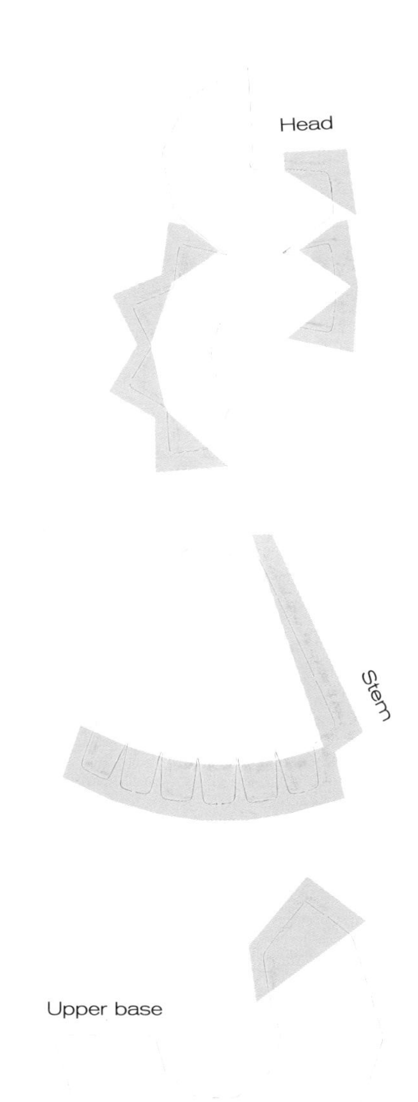

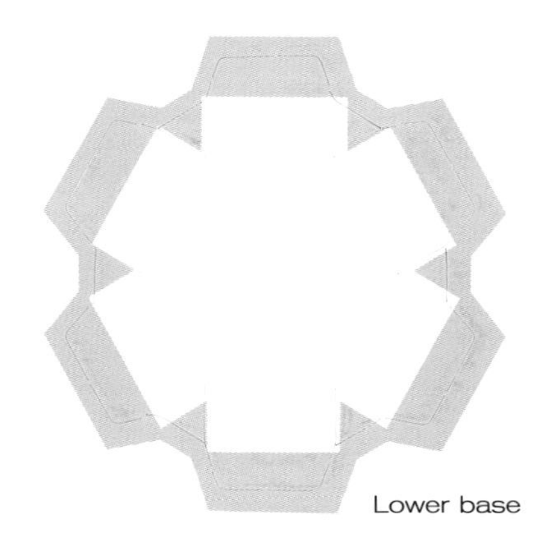

Spare White Pawn 8

The White Bishops (second set)

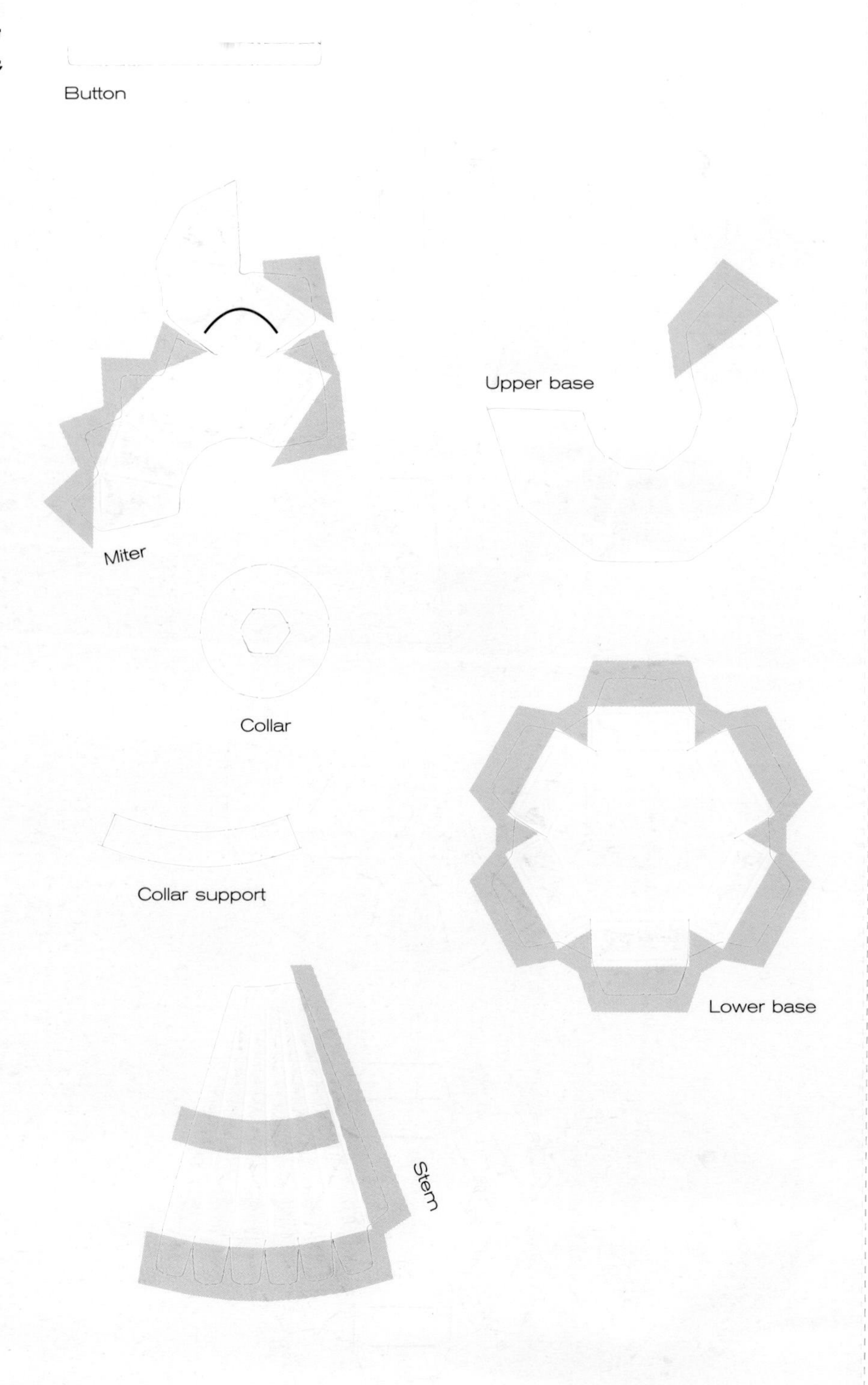

Spare White Bishop 1

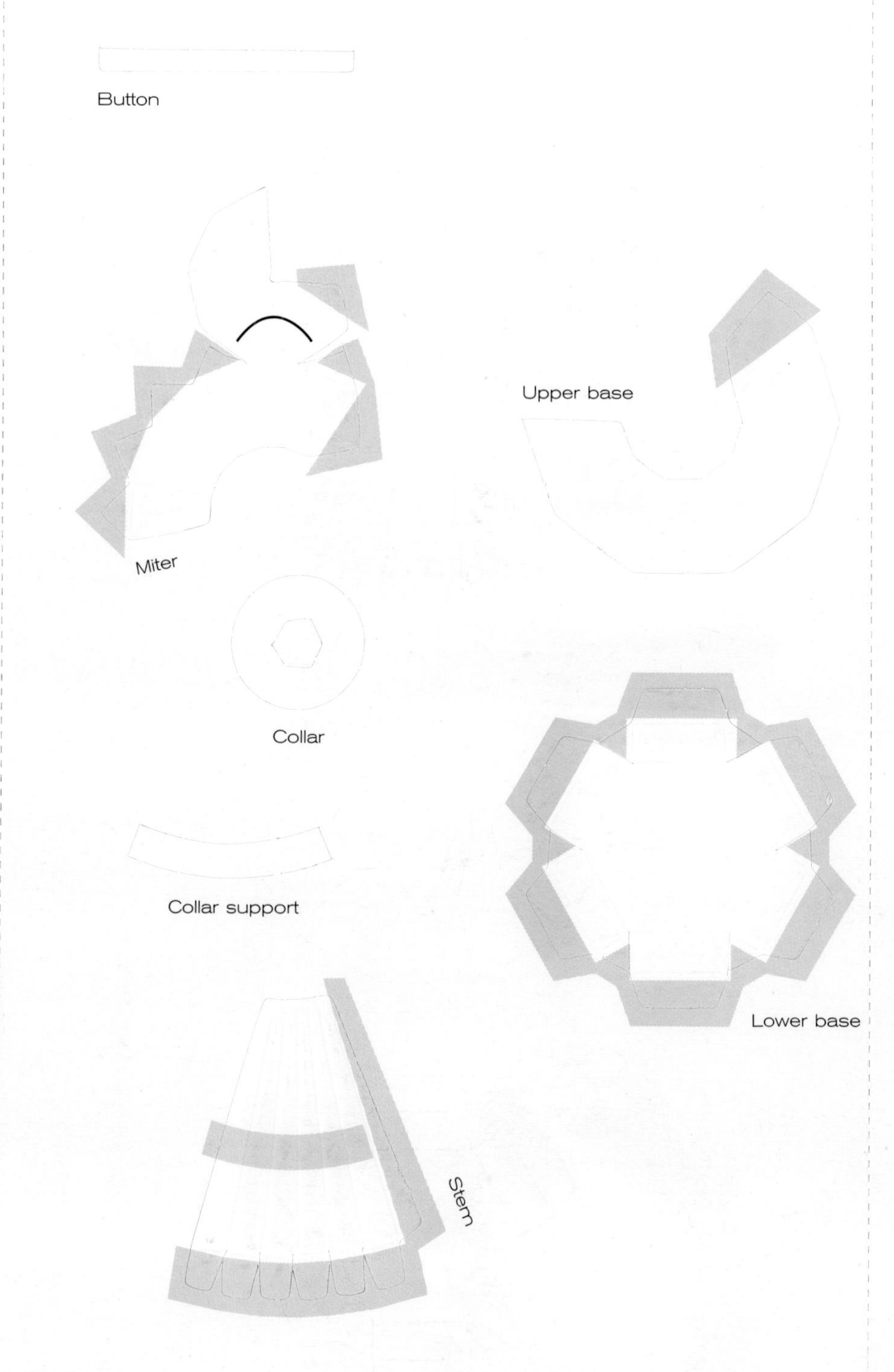

Spare White Bishop 2

The White Knights (second set)

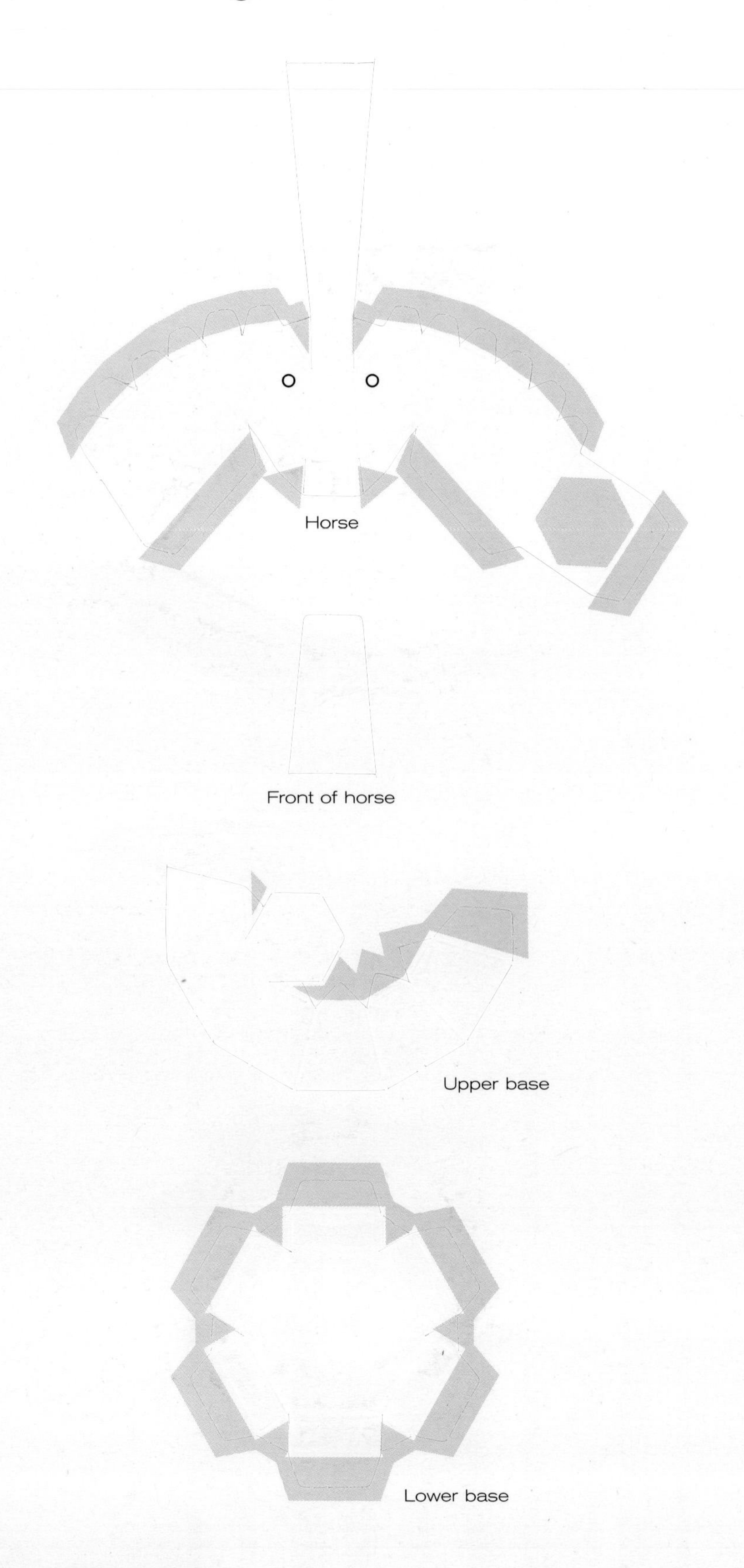

Spare White Knight 1

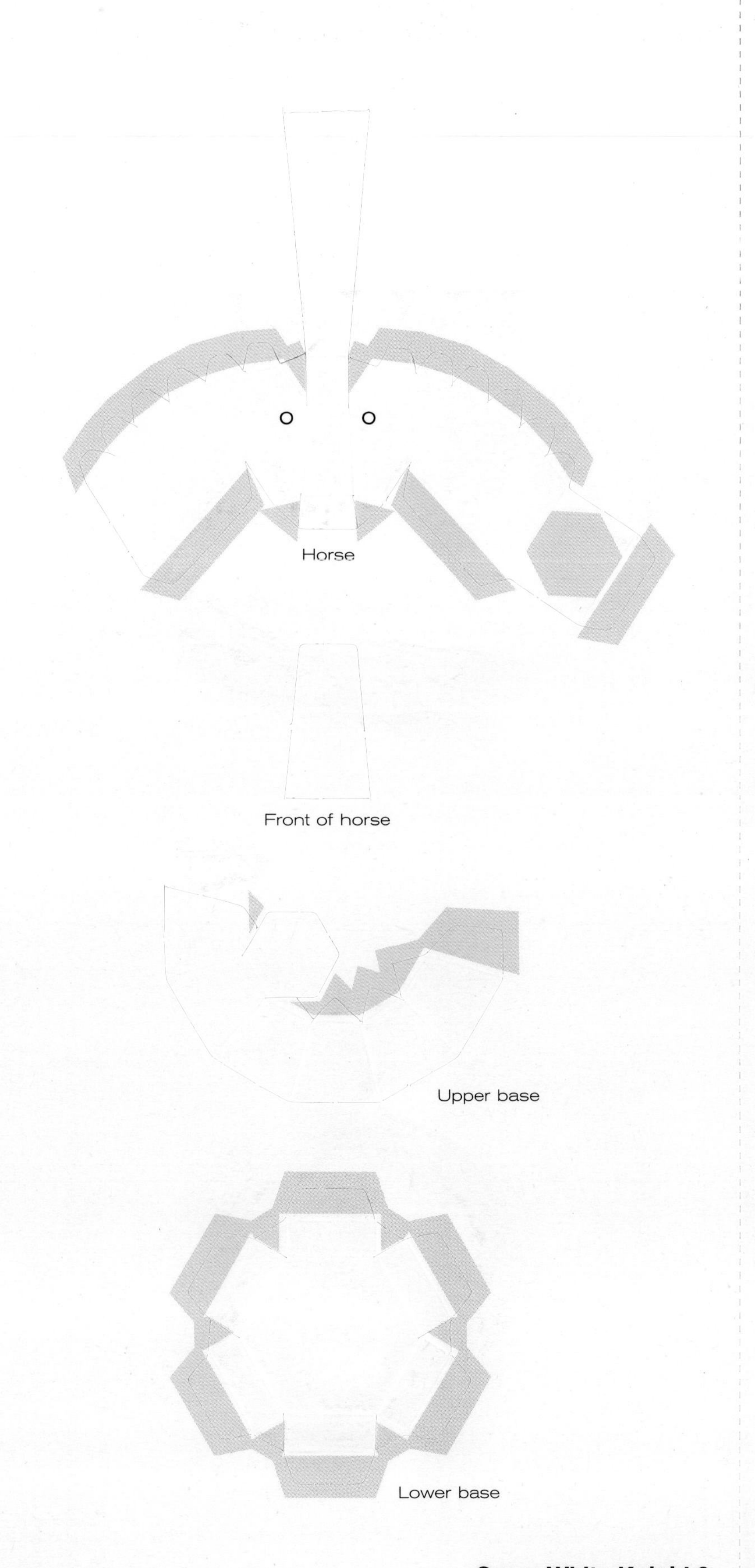

Spare White Knight 2

The White Rooks (second set)

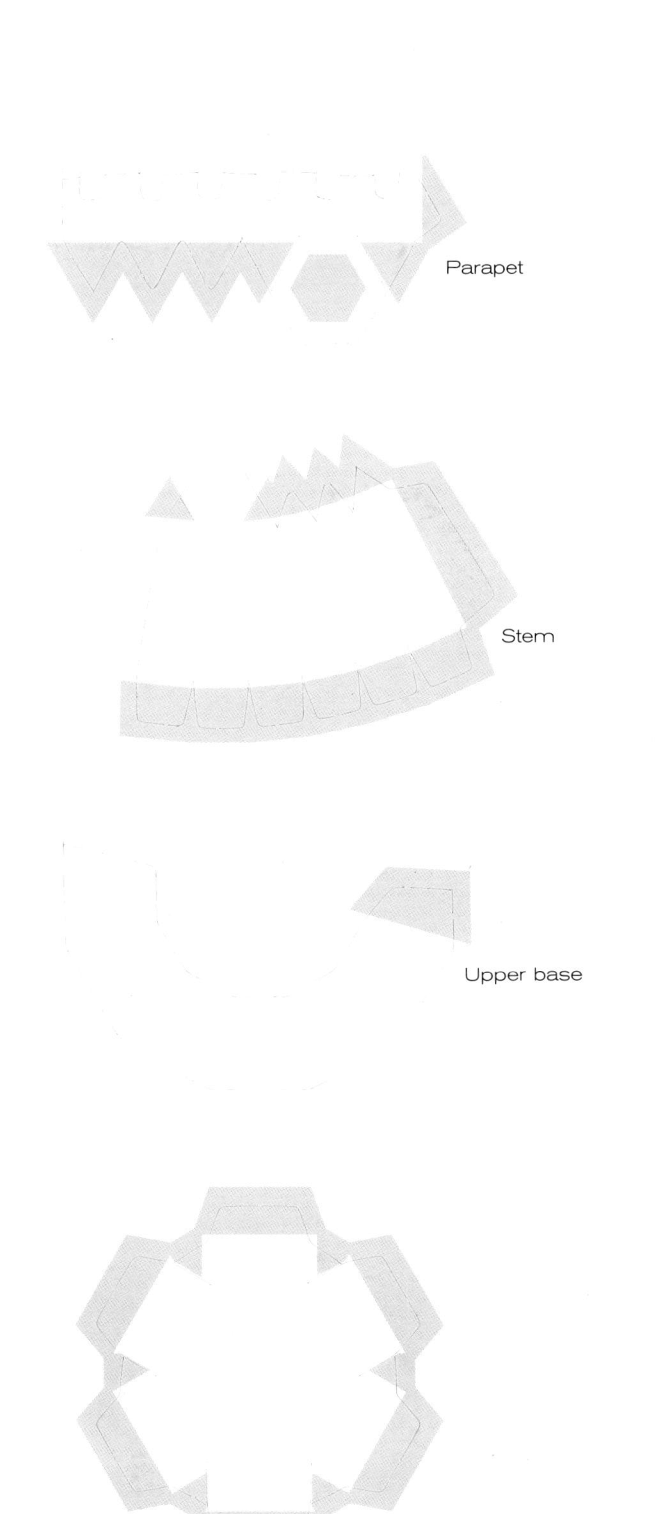

Spare White Rook 1

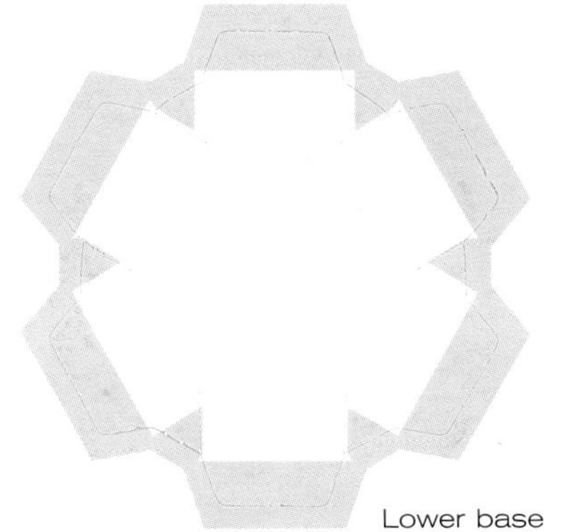

Spare White Rook 2

The White Queen & King (second set)

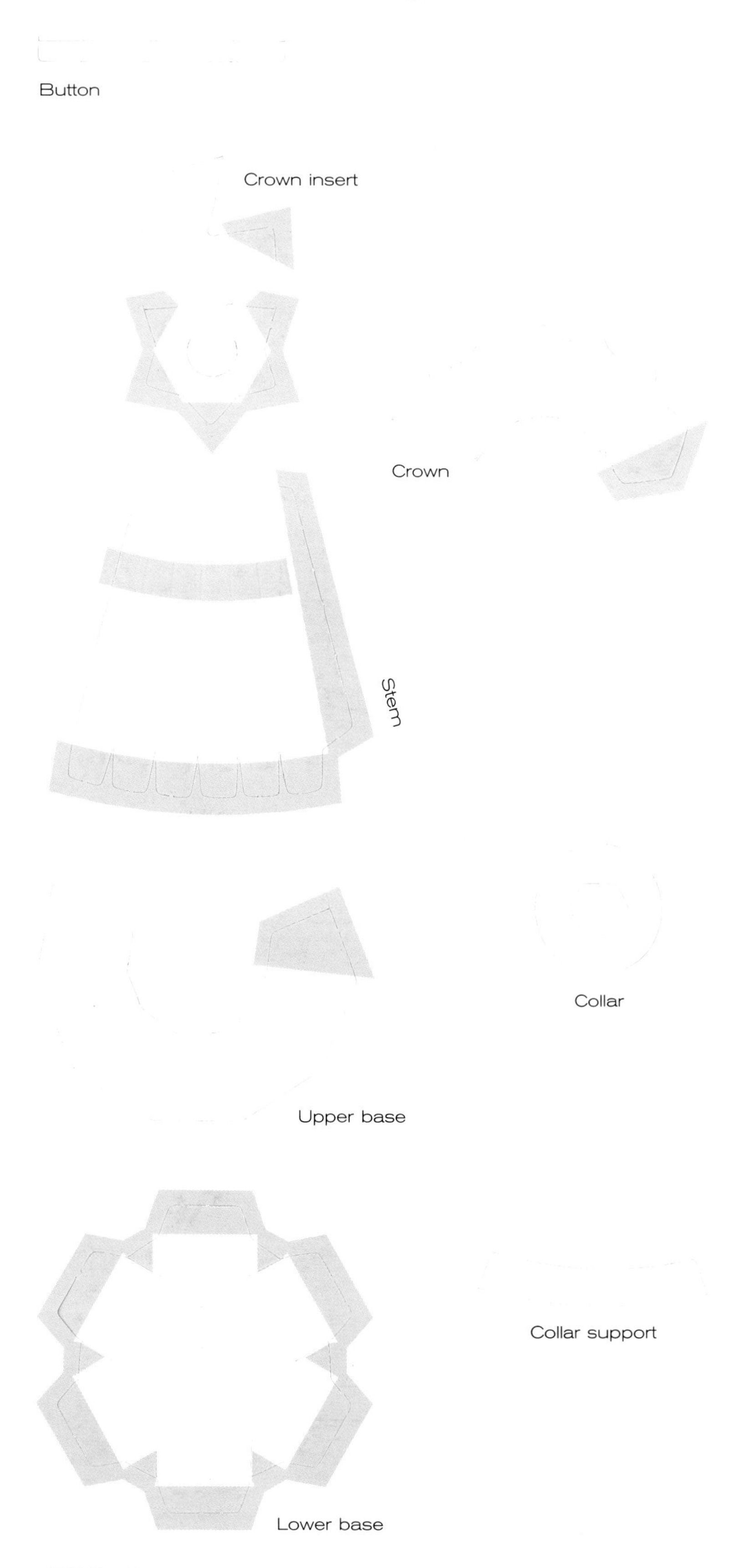

Spare White Queen

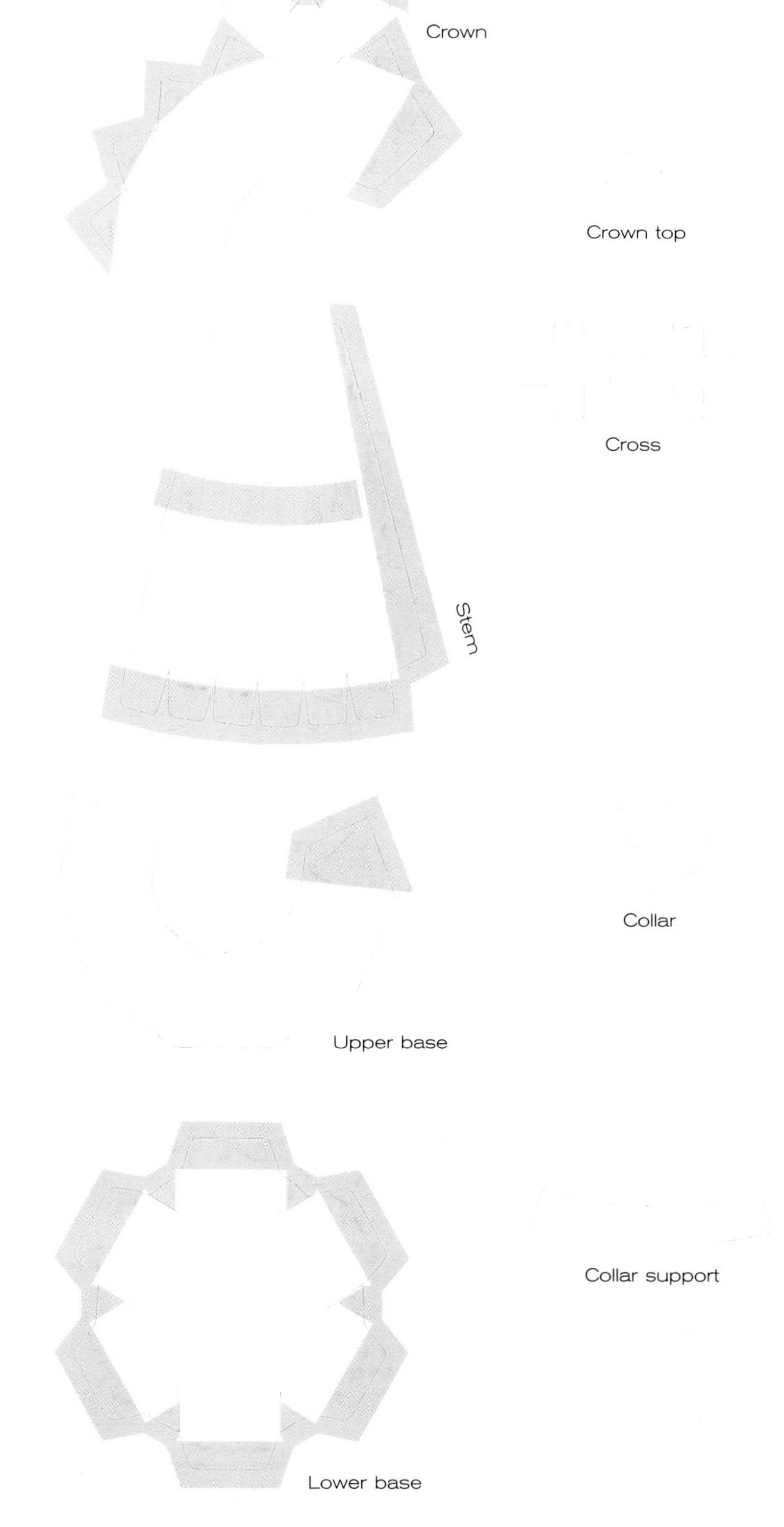

Spare White King

The Black Pawns (second set)

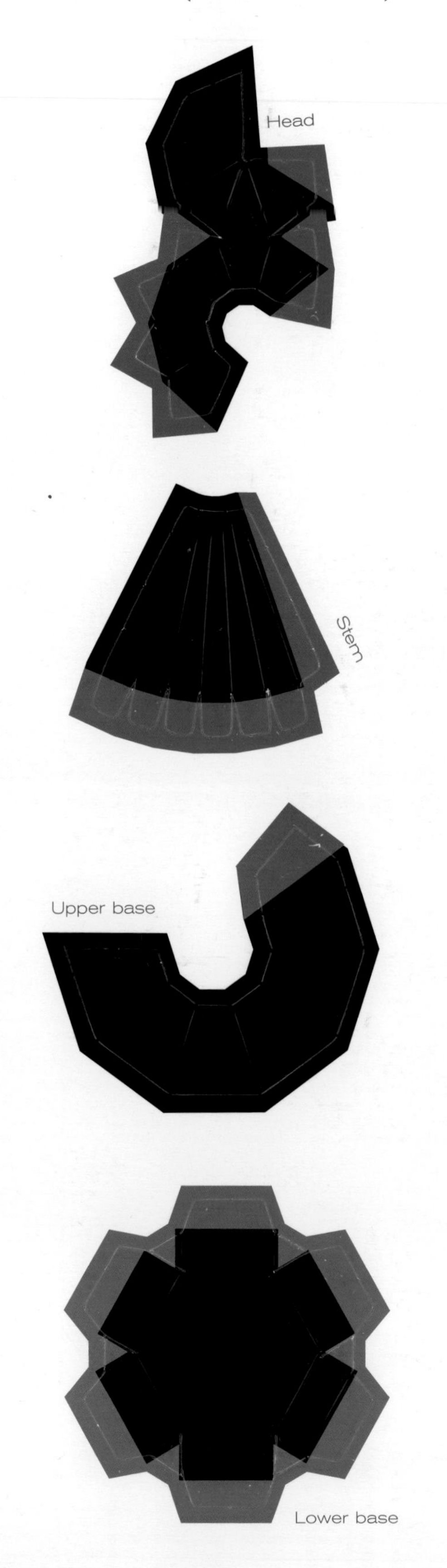

Spare Black Pawn 1

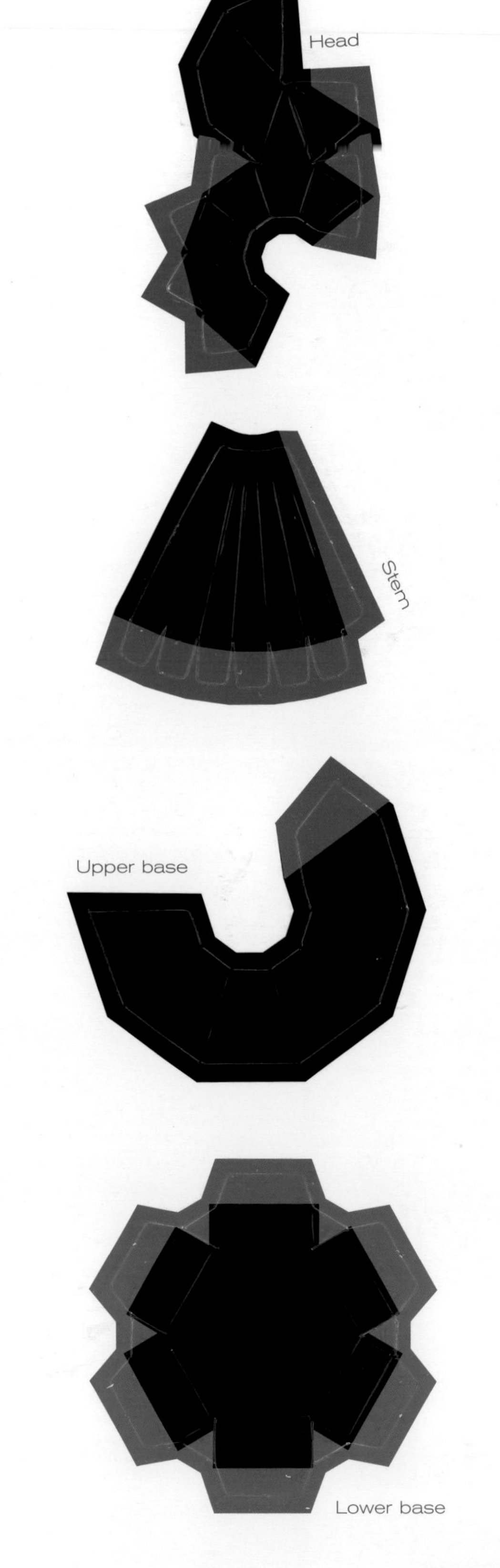

Spare Black Pawn 2

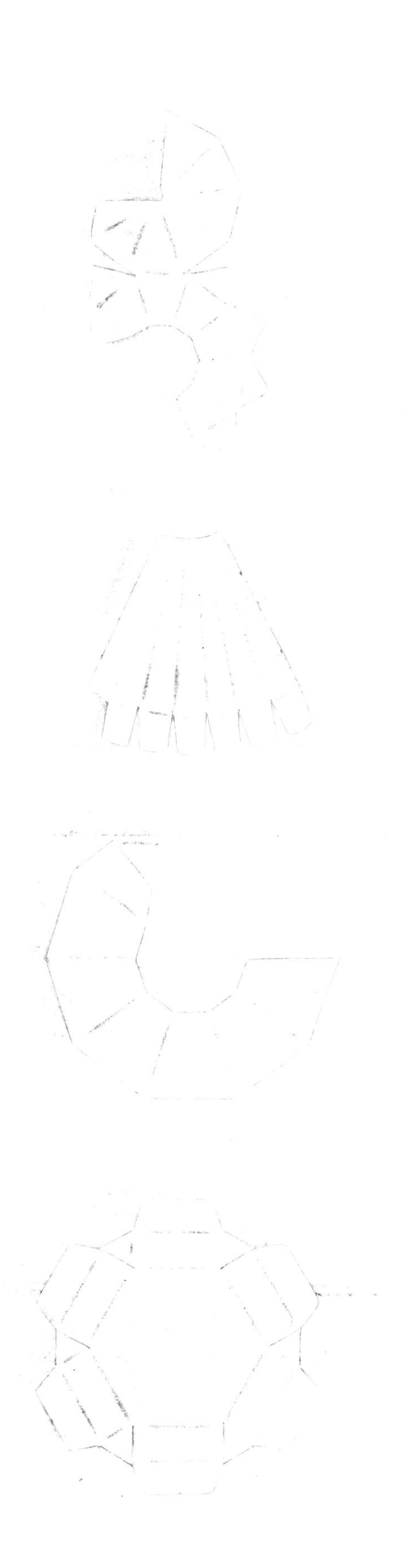

The Black Pawns (second set)

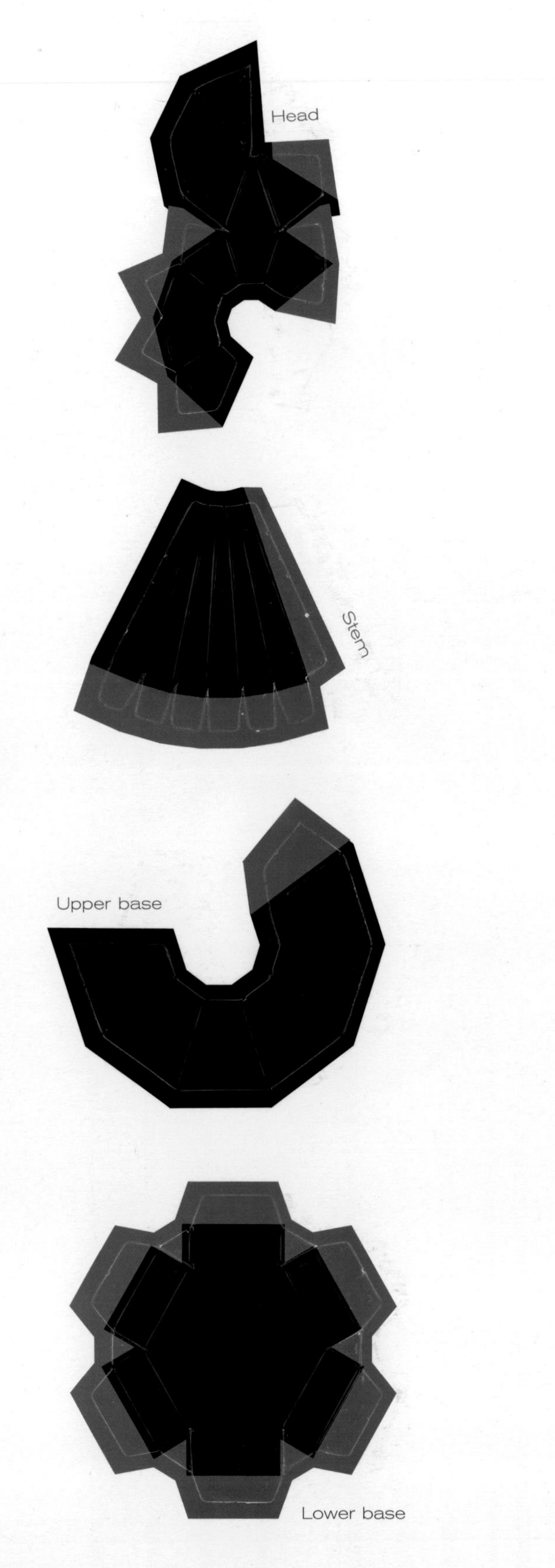

Spare Black Pawn 3

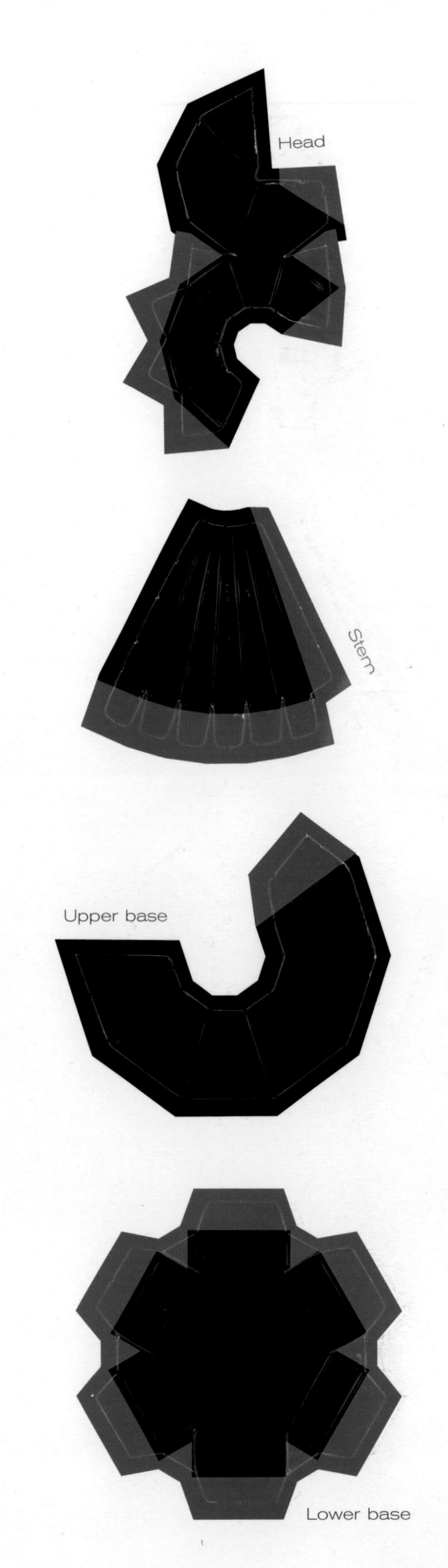

Spare Black Pawn 4

The Black Pawns (second set)

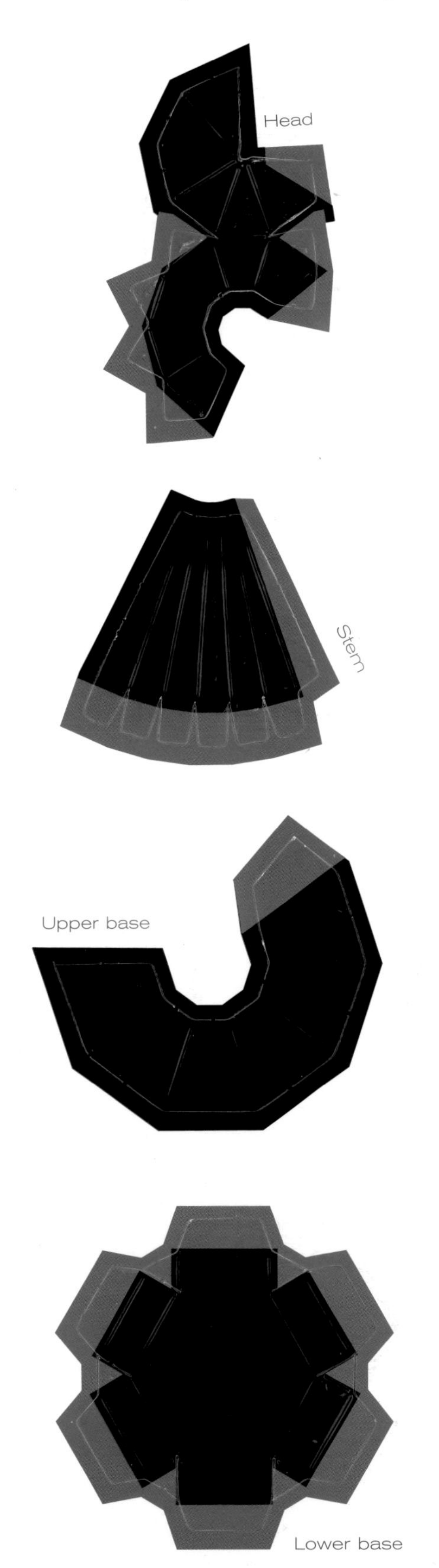

Spare Black Pawn 5

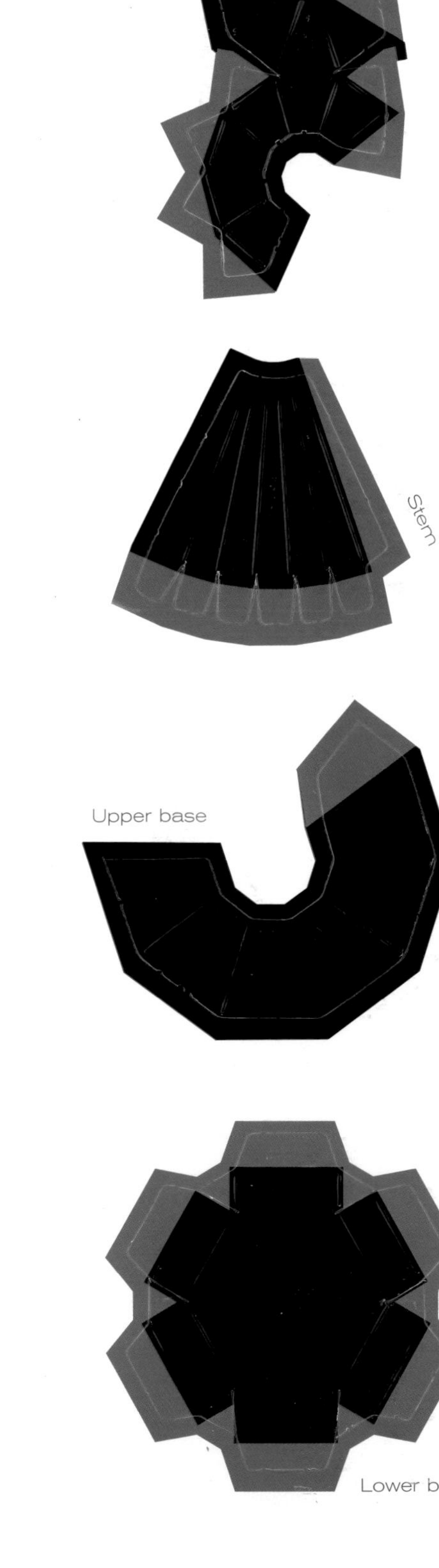

Spare Black Pawn 6

The Black Pawns (second set)

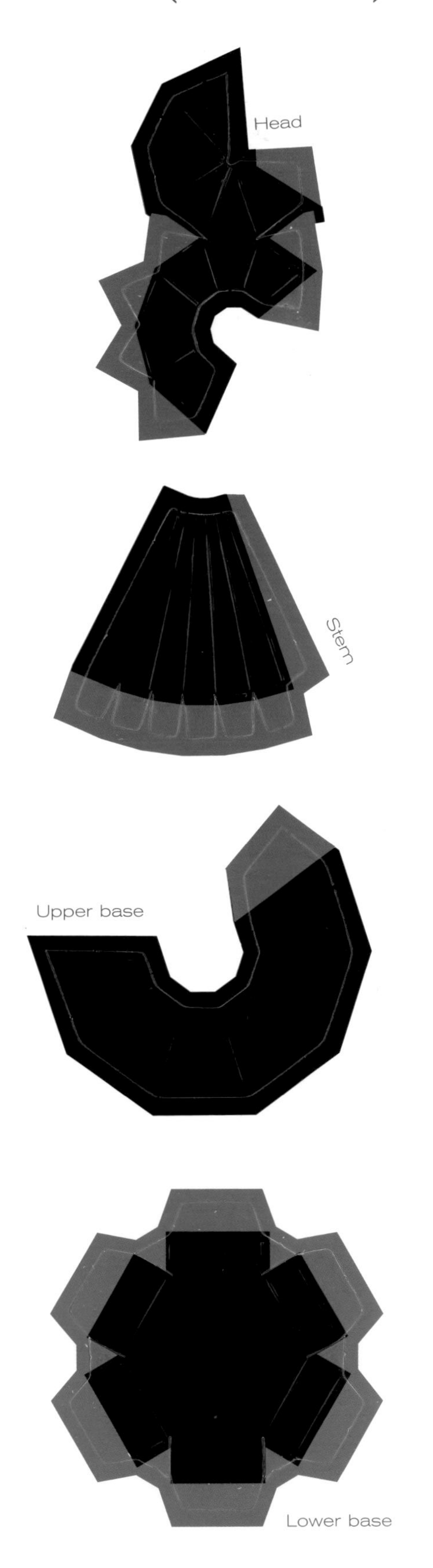

Spare Black Pawn 7

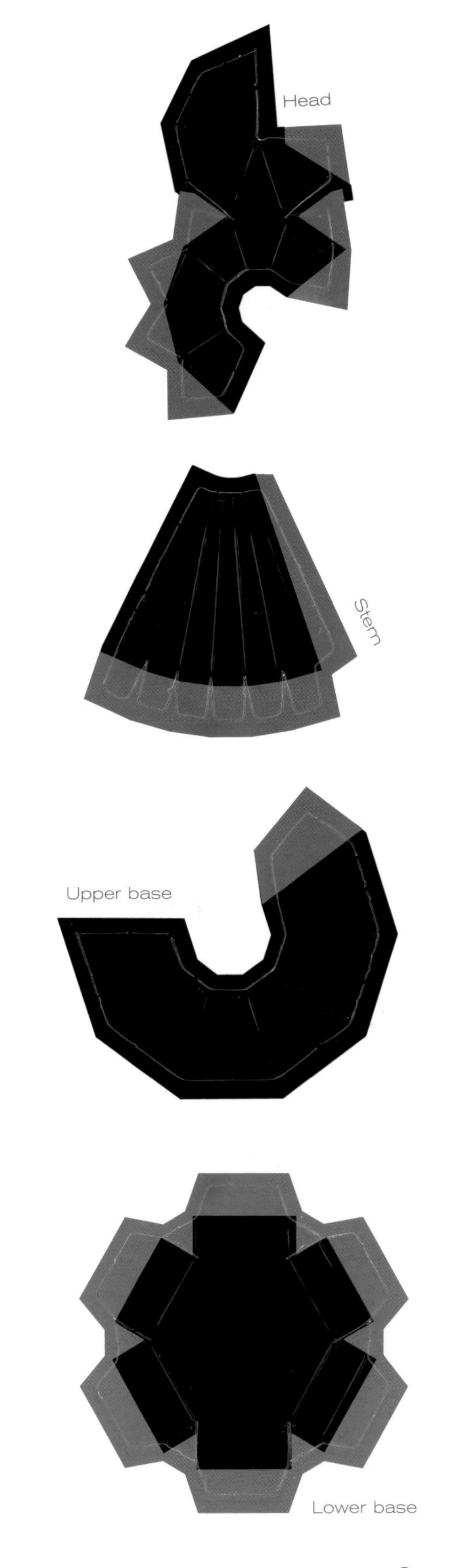

Spare Black Pawn 8

The Black Bishops (second set)

Spare Black Bishop 1

Spare Black Bishop 2

The Black Knights (second set)

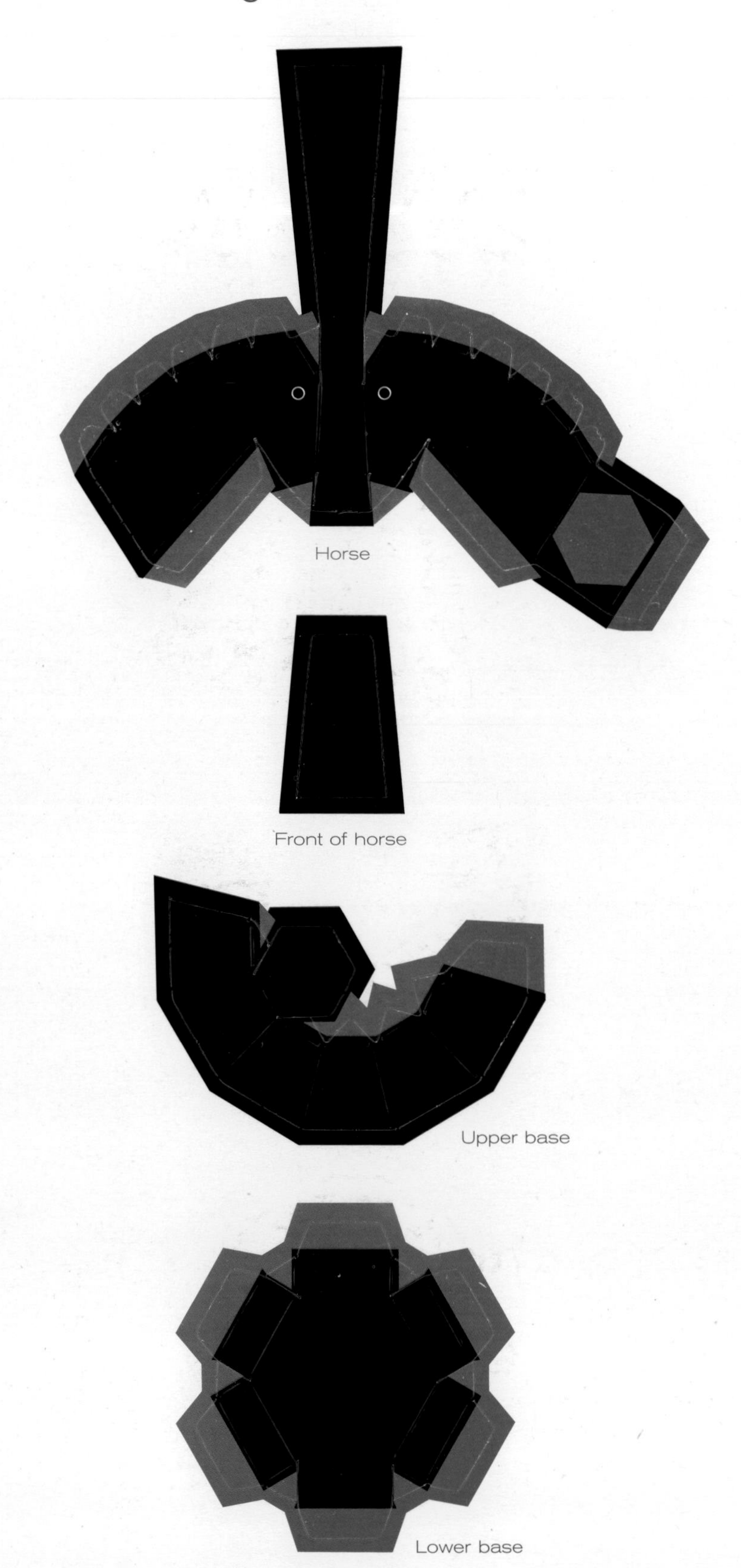

Spare Black Knight 1

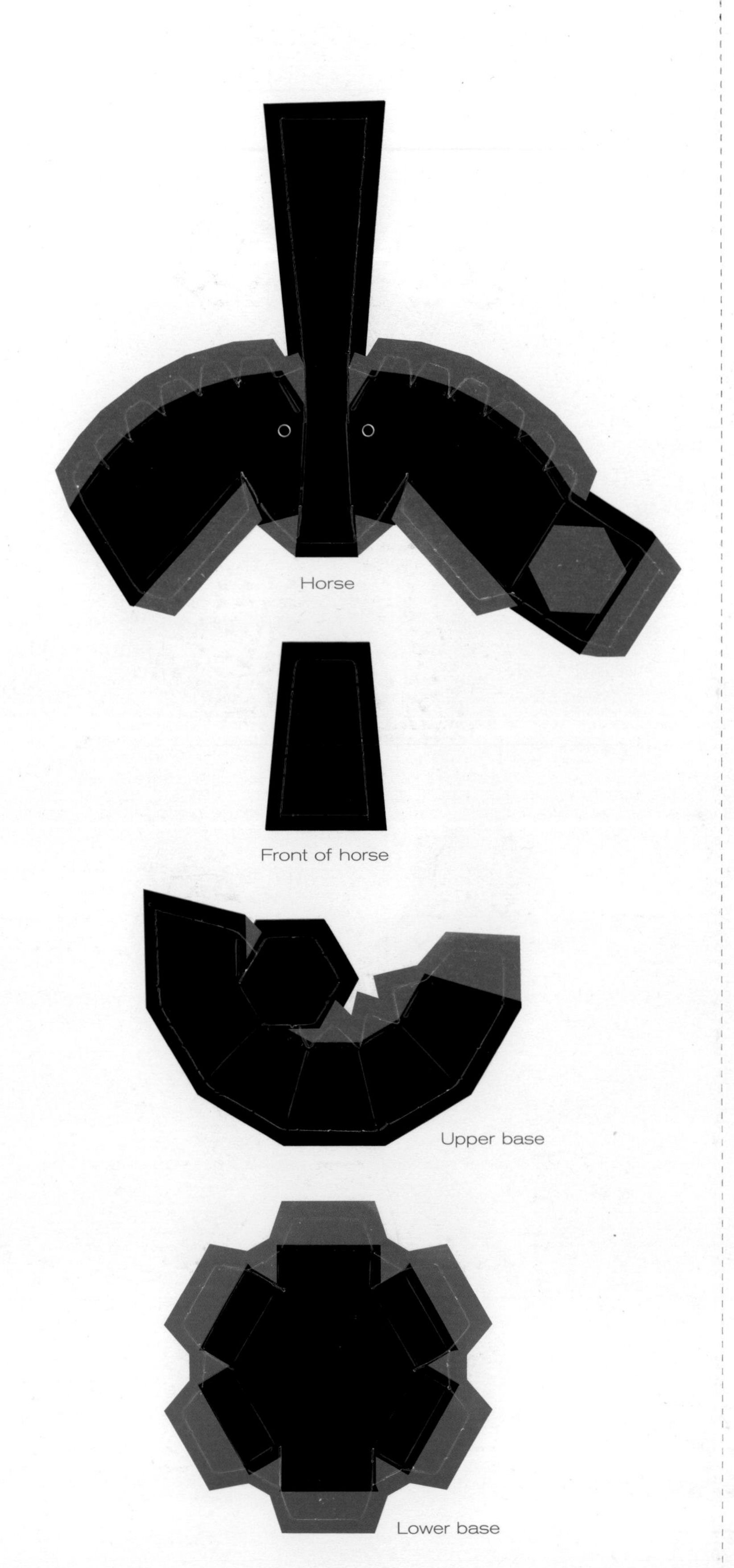

Spare Black Knight 2

The Black Rooks (second set)

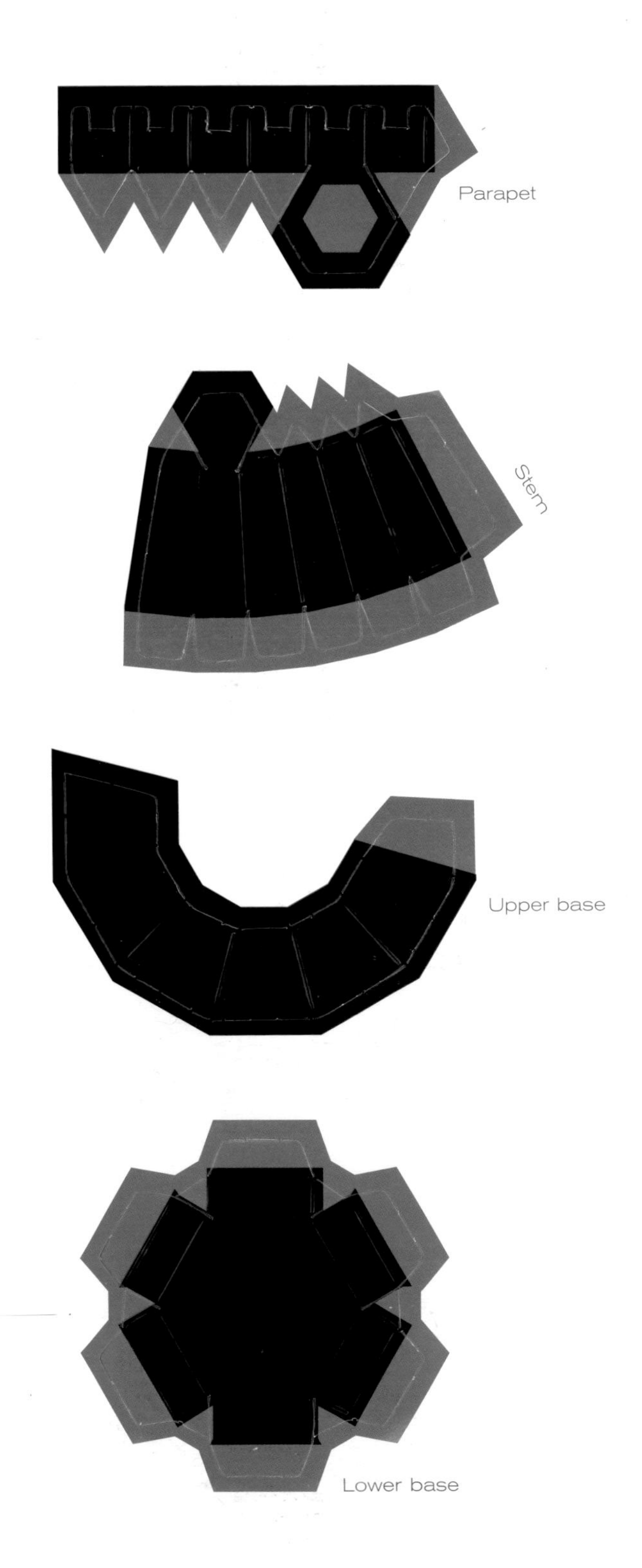

Spare Black Rook 1

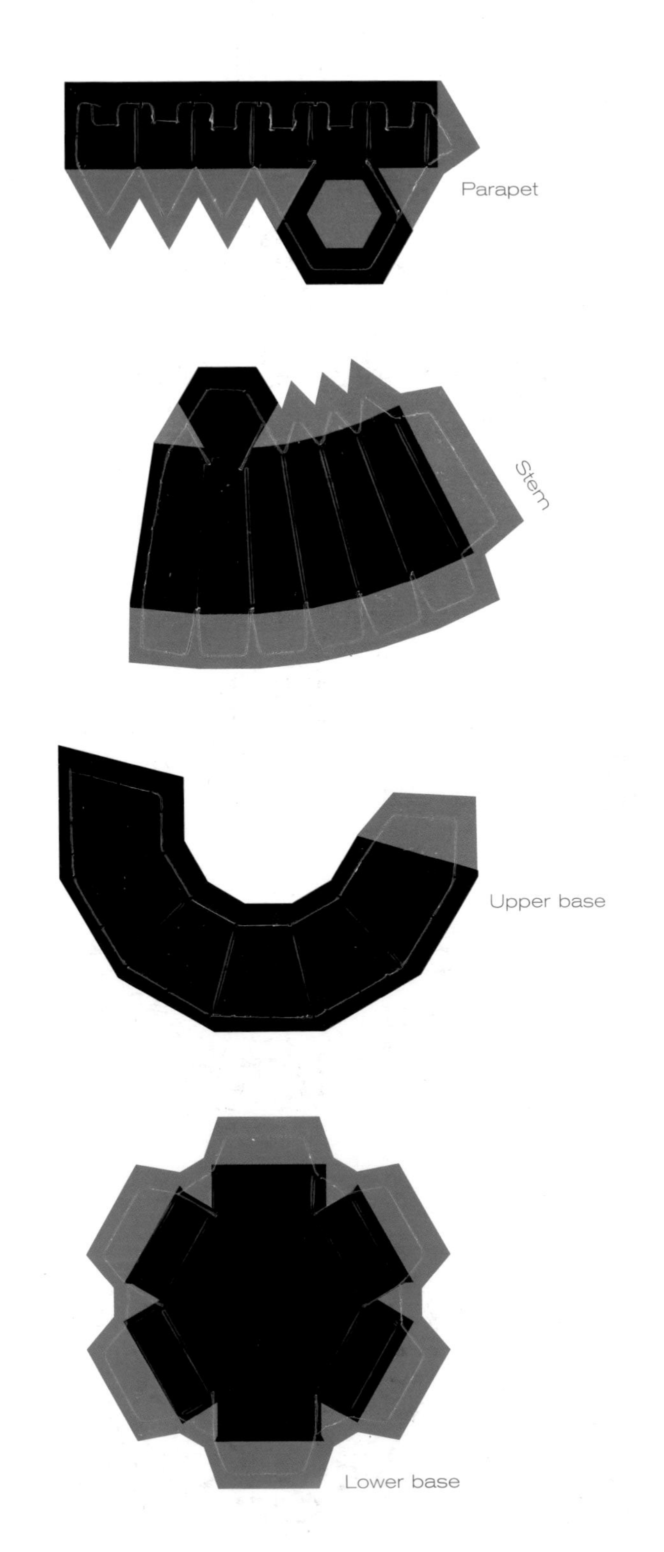

Spare Black Rook 2